Ped·i·cure

ISBN: 147818549X

ISBN 13: 9781478185499

Library of Congress Control Number: 2012912098
CreateSpace, North Charleston, SC

— torrid details of betrayal, sexual abuse, murder, suicide, emotional abuse, loss of parents, stalking, loneliness, divorce, addiction, self-doubt and numerous other situations which could have had unsuccessful endings; however, the outcomes will surprise and encourage all who read them.

Written by
**Mary, Gloria, Frankie, Cathy, Jill, Pamela, Ronna, Angela
and**
Katherine (posthumously 2010)

Table of Contents

Introduction

By

Jacqueline Feather

*O*n a warm Saturday in October I watched an animated group of women, none of whom I knew, tumble into the retreat hall at the Old Mission in Santa Barbara. I was leading a writing workshop to explore the hiding places of memory, and with a mix of curiosity and something bordering on suspicion, they set to work on exercises regarding Silence, Betrayal, and Desire. Later I would learn from Mary Beal Berchem how she had drawn these old friends together and organized this weekend so they could drop below the busy surface of their lives to explore their wild, wounded, and walled-off places.

In writing about memoir, writer Lyn Cowan, says the assumptions of cultural requirements and attitudes shape us, and each must contend with these archetypal themes and cultural forces. The task is to figure out what questions to ask, or even to recognize that there *are* questions. If we don't ask them then we recede anonymously into the collective psyche. Each of us has an obligation to let the future know what happened to us, to send our voice forward.

In my workshops, the first ingredient for such work is courage. Doubts and demons can keep a writer trapped by injunctions not to betray or break a familial silence, so as part of the evolving process I encourage everyone to read at least one piece aloud to the group. This can be a challenge, yet it often illuminates memoir work and connects body to word to voice.

Over the day, each woman in the group came forward, whether tentative, easily, or dallying behind Southern humor. One by one, their stories stilled the room. Over time, the group supported one another, shared secrets, stories…and kept writing. Aware they were not 'professional writers' they were, nonetheless, audacious, resolute, and quietly resilient.

"Regardless of how statistically similar our stories might sound, the details of each are unique," Mary describes of her own touchingly powerful story. Each of the women of *Ped·i·cure*, has dared to speak, to mend holes in the fabric of lineage and loneliness. Weaving connections between what was shut down, shut off, shut up, and allows a life to become a more open, breathing organism.

Pamela Bjork's *She Walked in Beauty* unravels the heartfelt depths of her sister's illness and suicide, while Ronna Brand stitches a lighter thread through friendship lost. "Makin' things nice," to keep her fragile mother out of the Hospital, Angela Johnston observes the poignant repercussions to her own soul; Jill Stouffer wrestles her dismay at colostomy bags and the deeper struggle of mothering her Mother; Catherine Muldoon's long dance with her estranged father and his distrusting wife captures the desire to repair damages of distance; Gloria Morrison's seemingly perfect childhood leads her into the shadows of addictions and breakdown, before break-through; Frankie Boyer poetically weaves the spirit of her dying mother with her own need to know, in their fragile last moments, she was seen, and loved. The final piece, by Mary Beal Berchem, is a tribute to her friend, Katherine, who died in her early seventies having kept her difficult childhood secret, noting thoughts and conflicts on small cards, but telling no one until a matter of weeks before her death. The book ends with her haunting question, written on a final note card: *What to do abt my voice?*

What the women in *Ped·i·cure* have done is send their voices forward. Reading each journey, I find myself moved and respectful. Each has taken the risk, dropped into familial, cultural, and personal silence and dared to swim the murky, sometimes painful, waters of memory. They have lived, suffered, sacrificed and, thank the gods, carried their scars with humor and earthy wisdom. They have claimed their own ground by telling their truth, as they invite you, the reader, to leave the cultural highway and find your own road home.

Preface

By

Mary Beal Berchem

*C*reating a bucolic autumn scene from tiny pieces of cardboard cutouts shaped like flat-headed gingerbread men is not my idea of fun. With over 520 unappealing choices on television, I'm bored and screwing around trying to finish this goddamn puzzle. No doubt, I will have a stiff neck in the morning, and this numb gluteus, adds to my frustration. Having almost filled the faded old red, covered wooden bridge and discovering a piece missing, *that's it*. Puzzles are not and have never been a pastime I enjoy; however, analyzing and trying to figure things out fascinates me. My favorite word 'why' was an enormous annoyance to catechism and schoolteachers, especially my prissy home economics teacher– damn I hated her.

While putting on makeup this morning, I *spazzed*, startled because the face staring back in the *now necessary* 10X magnifying mirror was, my deceased Mother's, not mine! The bright light streaming in from the bathroom window and those awful overhead fluorescents causes some distortion, but there she was with those sagging jowls, parenthesis lines on either side of her mouth, and deep creases over her top lip caused from years of sucking on *Marlboro's*. *Shit, what is this?* Blinking and trying to refocus *my* hazel eyes, not her pale baby blue, scrunching *my* nose and squinting for a more discerning look, no denying—her mouth. Cupping hands on either side of my neck; a breath–reassurance, it wasn't her *turkey neck*...thank god. When I was little, I prayed, *Dear God, Jesus, the Holy Spirit and Blessed Virgin, don't let me have her flabby neck!*

Where did this apparition come from? I've worked so hard not to be like her. Why now?

Wondering if any of my friends have had this experience, I left the bathroom without finishing; barren face, no blush or mascara making a beeline to my office — *Crap, where did I put it?* Relieved to have spotted the blue cover of the *Flavia* address book stuck among the oodles of paper in the two-tiered file, I pulled it out and glanced at the cover. The word — *Wonder* and two kites flying in the breeze struck a serendipitous chord. Perhaps there was an omniscient hand guiding me to the women who will understand my plight and tell me what I desperately want to hear: don't worry, you're not alone, it's okay. *Who do I call?*

Magically, names danced off the pages as if already choreographed; however, my enthusiasm dampened reaching pre-recorded messages...blah, blah. Within a couple of days, the phone started ringing. It had been years since I'd spoken with some, weeks with others; we all agreed, it felt like only yesterday. All they knew about one another was what they heard from me. The extra days prior to returning my call proved a blessing, I devised a plan: I will invite them to join me in Santa Fe for a girl's weekend. *I know they'll like each other. Besides, Angie and I have homes there, and plenty of room for everyone.*

It took a little convincing, maybe a hint of propagandizing, but everyone agreed. I was thrilled, *was it luck?* Nah; something else was happening. I assumed they'd love each other as I love them. When my eagerness subsided, I hoped I wasn't courting disaster; my overzealousness in the past proved such. There will be some awkwardness. Perhaps if we all write a *Tapa*, disclosing a small secret, any tension might ease. "Sure how long and how many words?" They replied. *Unbelievable.* I too would have to fess up...

We arrived at The Ghost Ranch Santa Fe Conference Center, located a block from the historic downtown plaza and named after Georgia O'Keeffe's, Abiquiu ranch. We couldn't have wished for a more beautiful morning. *So far, my hunch was right;*

they like each other. Someone suggested we take a group photo and the courtyard seemed a perfect backdrop with its giant black metal sculptures of cows, ostriches, ravens and elephants–*good luck fetishes*. I follow Native American beliefs that animals are sacred and carry ancient wisdom–a portent of what was beginning to unfold.

A few months before our meeting, I was sorting through old photos and ran across a black and white *Kodak* with the squiggly edges taken in the early 1950's in my hometown park in Clarkdale, Arizona. We were cute girls, Brownie Scouts, gathered and awaiting a field trip to Montezuma's Castle, a cliff dwelling near Camp Verde. Everyone had on rolled up blue jeans and plaid button down cotton shirts. Some wore brown cardigan sweaters, and everyone secured their Brownie beanies with *Bobbi* pins. Like a broken record, the photo played incessantly in my mind–*somewhere in our hearts, I believe we're still the innocent essence of those girls, smiling and standing tall, brown paper- bag lunches in hand, and ready for the field trip through life*.

Native American scenes of Kokopelli and Corn Dancers adorn the walls of the lobby. Nearby, a bevy of new visitors chat, rubbing their hands in front of the blazing piñon fire trying to shake off the early autumn chill.

"Hi ladies, ready to go to your meeting room? Follow me." Our pint-sized docent, more like a drill sergeant, waved her hand and we followed lock step. "Here we are, let me know if you need anything."

The room, larger than I'd imagined, smelled like brewing coffee and cinnamon rolls. A harvest gold and burnt orange tablecloth covered the serving table, and on top, a round aluminum tray piled with melon balls, pineapple, and berries. We dug in.

The tables were set for eight and everyone grabbed a chair. Each mother-hen musk marked her folding metal nest awaiting the laying of her egg.

Tapping my water glass trying to interrupt the flock, reminded me of fourteen deer-in-headlight eyes. *Who would think, the faces of women in their fifties and sixties would look like panic-stricken first graders asked to stand in front of class and read?*

"Pam, you're first," Jill said as if reading a "has the jury reached a verdict" pre-made note.

"I have a secret that's haunted me for years," she said in her usual soft, deliberate voice.

Everyone's interest piqued.

"I loved the vintage posters on the walls of the café in Denver where I worked. Especially, the gossamer skirted, bare breasted one reminiscent of a Toulouse Lautrec. After my brother's shocking death, I shamelessly asked a cohort to steal her for me; but I never hung it fearing I'd be outed as the thief! A few years ago, my sons and I uncovered it while scrounging in a forgotten area of our garage. *Guilty, I'm guilty!* Feeling embarrassed and with that creeping warm I know so well–*insidious*, menopausal night sweat, there is no shelter, no bed providing me refuge."

Pam drew my name.

"Mom made me go to confession every week. No way would I tell the priest I masturbated. So, I told him I ate meat on Friday and hated her, mortal sins too, but playing with myself, never."

In a genteel North Carolinian manner, Angie described her brother's horrific death. "The smell of vomit and other body fluids have never left my mind."

Stillness enveloped the room, perhaps a sniffle or throat clearing while the others read their equally compelling stories.

No doubt, we are novices, unprepared for this ride–amateur architects looking aghast at blue prints of a glass house, one we agreed to build. Transparency is the rule. No closet doors hiding shame, guilt, sorrow, fear or embarrassment. Assuring our bond, we locked pinkies and became friends like no others.

We continue our journey with hope and gratitude, and if by chance you're inspired to tell your story, your truth, your voice might also reach out and touch someone.

Life is full of puzzles and the entire picture not complete until the last gingerbread man fits.

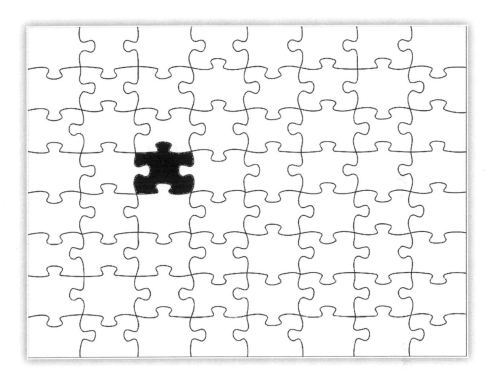

MAY   5 5

Brownies, 1955
"Field trip through life!"
Mary – 2ⁿᵈ from left, Cathy – 4ᵗʰ from left

Angela Johnston

I was born into a prominent Southern family of wealth and despair. If you met me, you'd never know the kind of life I had growing up. It was perceived flawless and carefree, one to be yearned for. When I was a child, my joy and laughter were contagious, and full of Polly Anna visions, very different from what was really taking place. I decided when I was very young to make the best of life, live each day with hope, embrace joy not sorrow, laugh instead of cry, stand up when knocked down, and reach out rather than withdraw. I made good choices and bad choices, but that's just life. I have five children, and twelve grandchildren, two stepdaughters, and six step-grandchildren. I'm an artist/painter; I sell and paint commissioned work. Jim is my second husband and we live in Morrisville, North Carolina and Santa Fe, New Mexico.

Secret Keeper

By

Angela Johnston

*S*eptember mornings in North Carolina can be muggy —
air so heavy I lie in bed wearing only a white cotton tank
top, relishing the cool breeze from the ceiling fan and sipping
sweet iced tea. The weatherman reports another steamy day with
a heat index in the 90's. I chuckle remembering Mama's lovely
euphemism "Makin' things nice," said ever so often when I
was little and complaining about being hot. I know she's right,
and when the snow and biting winds of February begin, I'll be
wishing for this heat.

*Damn, I hate talkin' on the phone this early, maybe I'll just let it go
to message…no, I better answer it.*

When I pick up the receiver, an unfamiliar guttural moan
startles me, sounds a little like a wounded animal. *Must be a prank
call?* But, before I could hang up, a loud, terrifying scream shoots
from the phone.

"Whoever you are, I don't like your joke. What do you
want?" I demanded and listened a little more intently. There's

more and more screaming, then something—a hint, small but unmistakable—Mama?

"Mama, Mama, is it you, are you there, Mama?"

My heart pounding and fear rising from the bottom of my feet, shaking and trembling—*is this what we've been afraid of? No, no, I've tried to keep that tucked away in the part of my brain where unpleasant thoughts and feelin's go.* "What's wrong?" I pleaded, "Tell me." Dreading…Charlie…*no stop thinkin' that way, just put it out of my mind, and it will go away.* Everyone in the family's worried because his binges are frequent and though we may not have said it out loud, "he's *killin'* himself," it is indeed a grave possibility.

Taking a deep breath, I pushed the caller for more even though I was afraid to hold the receiver any closer. Then, more moans and screams turned into a sound I've never heard before, or want to hear again: wrenching pain from deep inside, as if one's soul was being ripped out.

Finally, I heard, "He's dead."

"Oh god Mama, no, hold on, I'm gonna find out what's goin' on. I'll have the Jarvis' over there in a flash, we'll get through this."

Charlie, thirteen years older—'my big brother'—beloved by all: tall and lanky with thick dark brown hair, cobalt blue eyes and a smile that could melt 'sinner or saint'. Handsome and he knows it. Daily, his model-esque designer attire, looks like he stepped out of *GQ*. His sense of humor leaves friends laughing and holding their sides. He is an omnipresent soul driving a vintage, gold cabriolet *Bentley* and piloting his own airplane, and for all his braggadocio has a generous heart. Years back, he was a successful hotelier and restaurateur. Food wasn't thrown out; rather, given to those in need, and many a time, rooms not booked were let to homeless folk. I wondered if his indiscretions were overlooked because of his caring and selflessness.

Memories flood my mind to another steamy summer afternoon. I was five. Natalie and Winston, my other siblings, were off playing with friends. Mama, Charlie and I were home. She needed to run errands and asked him to keep an eye on me.

Funny, how I recall bein' called a menopause baby, born almost ten years after the others.

Not sure where he was, I tiptoed behind the double wooden louvered doors outside the den. I tried being quiet, but he heard me. He was sitting in the Queen Ann chair looking out the window. All of a sudden, he turned around with that ornery grin and said, "Let's play."

"I don't wanna play, Charlie, I don't like your game."

Then he stood up, and I could see he was bare-naked. *Yuk, not again.* I was four when I first saw him playing with his weenie, making those weird noises and white stuff coming out.

"What kinda pee pee is that?" I wondered.

"Come on Angie, I want to play. Let's play," he persisted.

"No, no, no. I don't want to play." I said, louder and more adamant.

Then before I could run away, he lunges at me and misses; I escape his grasp and run through the hall, underneath the huge chandelier in the foyer, up the stairs, trying to get to my bedroom where I could lock the door. Reaching the first flight of stairs past the grandfather clock, I trip and he grabs my foot, my flip-flop flies through the air as I kick and struggle to free myself, but he pins me down and holds my wrists. I beg him to get off. The rough blue nylon carpet scratches my cheek as I flail; I can feel his naked body and penis touching the back of my leg.

Shouting, "Get off me, I can't breathe!" Thinking, *I wanna go outside and play,* but the words wouldn't come out of my mouth. Just then, I heard Mama scream, "Oh god!" Looking over my shoulder, I saw her standing right behind us on the stairs. I'll never forget how shocked she looked and how white her face was. Charlie jumped off and ran downstairs, she ran after him, and I followed.

I'm in trouble now, in trouble with him for lettin' us get caught, and in trouble with Mama for lettin' him do this to me.

He ran to his room by the den where she stopped him, yelling, "What did you do to her?"

"I'm sorry Mama, I'm sorry," he said staring at his feet.

"How could you do such a thing? Why, Charlie, tell me why?"

I was hiding outside the doors, frightened and not knowing what would happen next. He was shaking and crying, and tears were rolling down my cheeks 'cause I'd caused all this. Everything changed that day. My five-year-old sense of reasoning didn't know what happened except I felt bad, and it was my fault. I felt guilty and responsible for Mama's anger.

Soon after Mama caught us, she went to Highland Mental Institution and Charlie left for college. All I know was what we did was bad, and I had to go to the doctor. She wasn't like my other doctor, who looked in my ears, nose and mouth, she wanted to play puppets. They were strange, not like my dolls; they had 'private parts' and she wanted me to show her what Charlie and I did. I didn't play, and I didn't tell her nothin'. I'm not sure how long Mama was at Highland; when you're five, long could have been a week or a year, but it was too long. I overheard talk she had shock treatments, and I was never quite sure why she went to the mental hospital; no one ever talked about it. Therefore, I subconsciously blamed myself and for thirty-five years, kept it tucked away in what I call the *amnesia room of my mind*.

Back to Mama's terrifying screams coming from the phone.

"He's dead, he's dead!" she shrieked.

"Are you sure? Who told you this, Mama?"

I called the Jarvises, Mama's seventy-year-old next-door neighbors. Their bright blue wooden lake house is a stark contrast to Mama's bright yellow/orange trimmed cottage. I must have alarmed them 'cause I asked them to get over to her place fast, saying she can't be alone right now. But, I didn't have time to explain. Since Mama lives alone, I thank god for them keeping an eye on her. Most of the cabins on Lake Wylie are painted in rainbow colors, reminiscent of Key West, even though it's South Carolina.

Mama is a little bit of a woman, barely five feet, not thin nor heavy, carries herself well and I guess you could say her walk conveys self-assurance. However, many times I am confused by her moods—up down, constantly shifting–and I feel a need to please her, which is not necessarily well received. Nevertheless, she is my Mama and I love her. I hang up the phone, consumed with anxiety, hyperventilating, room spinning and feelin' like I had a huge hole right through my body — *what is this paralyzin' ringin' in my ears?* Grabbing the same clothes I wore yesterday, clam diggers and sheer white cotton blouse, I head downstairs to the garage. The phone rings and it's Red, my brother Winston's wife.

"God, Angie...he's dead, Charlie's dead," she said. Red's tall–almost six feet–large-boned, with freckled face and arms, and powerful head of rusty *Crayola* red hair. Her "comme ci, comme ca" attitude makes her a good partner for my "uppity" brother. Hysteria blocked any information I could get out of her. She kept yellin', and I told her I'd have to get back with her later. Composing myself was not easy, but I knew I had to call my niece Tiff, Charlie's beautiful twenty-year-old daughter. I figured she was at Charlie's house, and could tell me what happened. I truly was amazed when she answered the phone, her voice was cracking and she sounded scared. Apprehensive, I said, "Hi Sweetie, what's goin' on? Nana, just called...is it true? Are you okay?"

After a forlorn deep sigh, she said, "I went to Dad's this morning to feed the horses. I always go up to the house when I finish. I thought it was unusual no one was stirring about, so I yelled, "Hey, Dad I'm here. Where are you?" I went room to room looking for him; there he was, lying on his bedroom floor, face down in a pool of vomit." Silence overtook us for a moment. "Tiff, I'll be down as soon as I can get things together here."

Our home in Denver, North Carolina is an hour from my brother's farm in South Carolina and my husband Frank and I wasted no time getting on the road. When we arrived at the estate around nine a.m., a foreboding feeling washed over me as we drove through the open wrought-iron gates. The last time I visited, I had to stop outside and push a button on the intercom located in the brick stanchion, and Charlie unlocked them from inside his house.

For some strange reason I kept thinking, Mama owns the majority of the hundred acres, Charlie just about six. Giant Magnolia trees line the groomed dirt road leading to his house, and as we got closer, the size of his Georgian-style home, with its massive cream columns, amazed me, even though I'd been there before. There were cars in the circular driveway, a sheriff's and a white van with small hard-to-make-out black lettering on its open back doors. My brother labored to create an authentic-looking Antebellum home, not missin' a detail. He started living there soon after breaking ground and slept in the pole building, a metal garage and storage shop my parents built years ago when they had a tree farm on the land. He was diligent over every step of the construction and rarely left. For all I knew, he was consumed with his project, and I, a busy mother of five, didn't expect much in the way of communicating.

Opening the front door, a noxious blast hit me—grabbing my nose, I gagged from the stench of acidy bile and stale-smelling urine. *I wish Tiff had told me, but how could she possibly have described this?*

The stage was set, reminding me of a murder scene from a movie; puddles of body fluids congealed on the dark slate floor, and bloody handprints and swipes smeared all over the cream walls. An overturned and broken coffee table lay in the other room, its pine floor splattered with vomit. The living room walls were bloody from his falling against them, and hand prints were evidence of him trying to pull himself up and falling. Nothing seemed real. I moved slow motion, heart pounding and with this deafening ringing in my ears—I couldn't breathe! An aura of darkness surrounded two rather large men walking towards me, the bright light behind them make it impossible to see their faces. One man took my arm and said.

"Ma'am, you don't want to go in there; you don't want to see."

Tears poured from my eyes, I trembled, and stuttered, "I, I want to see my brother, I want to see Charlie."

What is this ringin'? I wasn't sure what was being said; the ringing in my ears muffled everything. The coroner's mouth was moving, but I couldn't make out what he was saying. I was in shock and my mind was racing. Then I got it.

"We'll be taking him to Harry and Brant Funeral Home in Charlotte. It's best you not see him now; let us clean him first," he said compassionately.

I hate this, I hate these men of death bein' here, why Charlie did you do this?

"Ma'am, will you come into the dining room, I need to ask you a few questions," the sheriff said lookin' stone faced.

Hollow, blank, void, endless, numb, forever–floatin' in and out of my body.

The doors to the bedroom open and clapping sounds from the gurney rolling along the wood floor and getting closer to the dining room fill me with anxiety. I saw an indistinguishable long object in a black bag...*Charlie!* The wheels bounced over the doorway and down the front steps. The solemn men pushed the death cart against the back of the van; the legs collapsed and they slid it inside, slammed the doors, and drove away. Standing in the doorway, we watch the van disappear down the dirt road, ease through the gate with our family crest and head to the main highway. *He's gone, Charlie's gone.*

Did I tell him what he meant to me? Did I tell him I forgave him? I'm the secret keeper; I never told anyone, not even Dr. Diamond who, for twelve years played puppets, trying to coax it out of me.

Frank and I return to Charlie's bedroom. *Thank god, the carpet is maroon; hopefully, the stains won't show. Mama will be here soon, and she can't see this,* I keep repeating in my head as I race around, picking up soiled clothes, righting overturned lamps and the antique mahogany side table from our family home. Incoherently stammering...*She mustn't see this, Mama I won't let you see this.* Finding a bucket in the pantry and filling it with disinfectant, I scrub, cry, and gag for what seems an eternity. *I've got to fix this.* The vile smell not only permeates my nostrils, but my soul. I try in vain to wash away the "dirty" thoughts, but my mind keeps resurrecting our naughty game. Vomit rises in my throat, and I swallow hard 'cause I hate puking. *Got to fix it, fix it before Mama gets here. She can't go back to Highland Hospital; that was when I lost her, when she walked in on us.*

My brother's elderly caretaker Jeff worked for Charlie many years and I am sure he's cleaned up messes and binges and god knows what. We agree there's no saving the mattress and bedding, so Jeff and my husband stack them and set them on fire. As the smoke rises into the air, I wonder what secrets the plume carries away.

We had to get things done quickly before Mama arrives, and I scurry about cleaning, and straightening, "makin' things nice." Jeff talks, as I never heard him talk before. He says he and the other workers knew about Charlie's afflictions and cleaned up after his "drunken stupors" 'cause they needed to keep their jobs. "We didn't tell a soul, Miz Angie, and there's sompin' else you should see," he said and motions for us to follow him into my brother's enormous closet. There were rows and rows of clothes: summer suits, linen pants, dress shoes, deck shoes, boots, and racks of ties. He stops in front of a lower rod full of starched cotton shirts, and, with his calloused, dark brown hands, slides them aside, then presses gently on the back panel and magically, a small door opens. An automatic light illuminates stacks of filthy pornographic videos and magazines and, higher up on a slender shelf, traces of white powder lines of cocaine.

Nothing could shock me after what I'd already seen; my heart couldn't be any heavier. Panicked that Mama would see this too, Frank and I packed two large boxes and put them in the trunk of our car.

Exhaustion overtook me; Jeff said he and the others could finish, "makin' things nice, befo' ya Mama gets here." Frank and I left and on the drive home, half-awake, I questioned my actions the months leading to his death. *Did I somehow let him down? Maybe, I should have called him more often.* The what ifs? Truth was I knew there was nothing I could have said or done.

Mama didn't go to the family estate until the day when those of us who loved Charlie gathered on a hill out behind his home to bid him farewell. A soft breeze carried the hollow tones from wind chimes he'd made in his metal shop.

For three nights after his death, I cried myself to sleep. On the third, I dreamed we were walkin' hand in hand around the farm and communicating telepathically. He looked like a shimmering white spirit. We went inside and sat on the living room sofa. I looked into his eyes and asked why he killed himself. "Your death certificate said you died of acute alcohol poisoning. How could you drink yourself to death?"

He answered by saying, "We all have choices, I made some destructive ones, sweet sister. I am happy now, and here I have peace. There is no pressure, just love. I saw how my actions affected me and my loved ones, and learned there is a better way, my demons are behind me."

I felt his joy, but had some apprehensions. Little pieces of information floated in my mind, things unanswered — unknown.

"I'm sorry I hurt you when you were little. I love you, and I'm sorry you've carried this secret in your heart all these years. Open that locked door someday and be free. Know that I love you and never meant to hurt you. I love you," he said, with loving eyes.

I felt peace. I could now let go of him and our terrible secret.

Several months after his death, Mama moved into Charlie's house, completing his vision. She said her memories of life lived well at the farm brought her peace. I knew she felt closer there to both Charlie and Daddy who'd died of cancer four years earlier.

Mama was eighty-nine when she was diagnosed with breast cancer. Soon after it went to her lungs, she chose not to see doctors or have treatment. She told me she didn't fear death; rather, welcomed it and longed to be reunited with her loved ones. Before she died, there came a time when we talked about the molestation; she wasn't sure who had done bad things to me. I feared too much discussion would tax her fragile mind. However, I knew I must clear the burden carried in my heart all these years. There could be no confusion.

"Mama, Charlie molested me, no one else." Ripples pulsed through me, shocked I'd told the secret. My heart broke seeing her eyes fill with tears. I did not want to bring her pain. Guilt began nicking away at me again. Then, suddenly, a powerful tsunami swept over me and carried the pestilence away, allowing me to realize I had dominion over my life. Now victorious, I could hold my head high. "Mama, he never meant to hurt me, he loved me and I loved him, I'm okay." And with those words, I regained my voice. Few people, if any, escape life unchallenged by pain, grief, sorrow or guilt. The choice of how to deal with it is up to the individual.

11

Light filtered through the sheer curtains, barely touching her face. Never before have I seen her so fragile sitting on the floral love seat in the "keepin' room." I had mixed feelings of love, sadness and compassion for my dear mother, and wondered — *did she comprehend what I'd told her?* It no longer mattered.

After she died, once again I was "makin' things nice," gathering her belongings stashed away for years under the stairwell. Christmas decorations, and whatnots and that portrait of me painted when I was five, wearing my favorite Sunday church dress–polished pink cotton and white lace. My pixie cut golden hair, and skin soft as butter. My heart stuck in my throat seeing those sad, tired, old-before-their-time eyes. Years earlier, the painting hung in our living room. I avoided looking at it. No wonder — those eyes told a story that has taken me fifty-two years to tell.

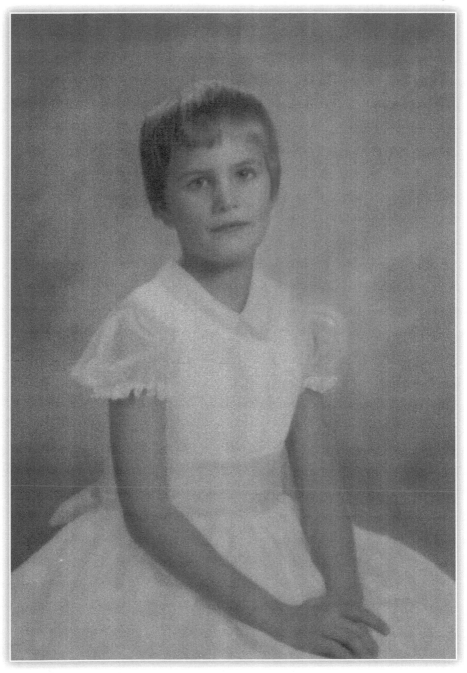

Angela, the portrait
"Those sad, tired eyes."

Epilogue

While typing and pouring out my heart and remembering things I've locked away for so many years, tears flow. I realize my breathing has slowed and the pounding I feel when I place my hand over my breast is unnerving. But, as I return to my thoughts, anxiety is replaced with a calm reassurance that I will be washed and cleansed of all this hidden pain and guilt.

Yes, writing about the pain and sorrow I've kept vaulted away, buried so deep, even years of therapy couldn't unlock was difficult. I remember feeling dread as I continued writing, then, as though a gift fell from the sky and landed in my thoughts, a verse from the bible flashed before me. "When I was a child, I spoke as a child, I understood as a child, I reasoned as a child, but when I became an adult, I no longer used childish ways." [1] I held on to that pain and carried the horrible secret throughout my life. After writing my story, I witnessed my soul's healing. Finally able to open up and give myself permission to set the pain and hurt free, I bathed in truth and forgiveness. The fragrance of an open heart sweeter than honeysuckle and lighter than early spring air, I was able to see myself clearly and embrace the woman I'd become. My only wish would have been for my parents to acknowledge I was okay, and to tell me they knew what happened and it wasn't my fault.

How could I, only five years old, betray my beloved older brother? The burden I've carried has at times been almost too much to bear. Looking back on what happened, there is no magic eraser, but the secret caused far more destruction than dealing with the unfortunate cause, which led to my abuse.

My story is about Love and Forgiveness — that is the only way I can truly be free.

Angela Johnston

---

1 Corinthians, passage, 11, King James Bible

Angela

Gloria Morrison

I was born in Utah, and cradled in love. We were Mormons and my aspiration was becoming a wife and mother. However, that goal became blurred after a disappointing first marriage, infidelity, alcohol addiction and contemplating suicide. After my family intervened, I crawled out of despair and found hope. I earned a cosmetology license and became a self-taught sculptor, making one of a kind character dolls, which I sell for thousands of dollars each. I have one son, two daughters, and four grandchildren. My second husband and I have been happily married twenty-nine years. I've renovated all our homes, bought and sold others for added income, and recently worked at *Target* supplementing our income. I also wrote a children's book, "*Wilbur's Wings*." We live in Placitas, New Mexico north of Albuquerque. The views from my windows are of azure blue skies, rolling hills, wide-open spaces and wild horses.

My Fall to Grace

By

Gloria Morrison

" *I* just want to fuck you!" I whispered in his ear after downing several *Tanqueray* on the rocks, erasing any inhibitions I would have otherwise. It was illicit, but I *did* want to fuck him.

Autumn evenings outside in the *Arizona Sonoran Desert* can be crisp. Our business club bash at *Old Tucson*, a western movie set south of town–chilly. Everyone gathered at a central location for cocktails and hor d' oeuvres, a 'meet and greet' before leaving on a chartered bus for the half-hour trip. Imbibing free liquor, many of us were well on our way to loopy, having no concern about driving or DWI's.

Harry, my husband, and president of the club told me he'd met the perfect guy– a Mormon, although jack Mormon, he wanted to 'fix up' with my younger sister, Peggy. "They'll have a lot in common," he boastfully touted. When this mustached, six-foot tall blond hunk, holding a beer in one hand and a cigarette in the other, walked up looking like no Mormon guy I'd ever seen, his seductive, blue eyes pierced my soul. I felt uncomfortable

19

standing next to my husband thinking, *Shit, can Harry sense the electricity between Bob and me?* I was immediately smitten and couldn't believe I was lusting after the very man my husband wanted my sister to meet. Passion struck, and filled us with desire; our body heat and language oozed—molten hot. I wanted to fuck him right there at the party. I don't know how we got away with kissing and petting to abandon with all the party goers milling around, but we were lovers encased inside an invisible bubble, mindless and oblivious, thanks to the open bar. My admission, seductively whispered in his ear, should have signaled *my* rock bottom, but I was only midway in a downward spiral. Later, he admitted my confession was his ultimate fantasy, manifest. He became my *paramour*.

My crisis of conscience came to a pinnacle that night; however, questions about why I'm here came the moment Mom pushed me from the womb. I didn't scream, "Waa, waa" but, "Why, why?" "Why am I here? Why do I have to believe what I'm told? Why can't I do what I want, where I want and with whom I want? Why are there so many rules?"

Fortunate to have arrived in paradise, I surmised God positioned me where I might be able to figure life out without strife or hardships, a home brimming with soft, gentle love, in the land of opportunity—the United States of America. With all the trappings of a carefree, blessed beginning, stereotypically, my life should have been easy.

My family, parents and three sisters belong to The Church of Jesus Christ of Latter Day Saints. Our Mormon lineage on Dad's side goes back to Joseph Smith. Mother's father was a convert, and when Grandmother immigrated from Scotland to Iowa and met Papa, she converted. Historically, the Mormon Church is young compared to many other religions. Mormons believe Joseph Smith communicated with God and Jesus early in the 1800's, found the golden plates, and proclaimed himself founder of, *the one true church*. In Sunday school, I learned Jesus loved me and we sang songs like, "Jesus Wants Me for a Sunbeam." My teacher encouraged us to live the word of the Lord. If I were disobedient, not following God's rules to the letter, I would not go to the Celestial Kingdom when I died, and that meant, *without my family for time an all eternity.*

I'm supposed to love Jesus. How can I love Jesus? I don't even know him. He died for my sins. What is sin? Was breaking Mama's new potted plant in half by accident, a sin?

The rules for salvation seemed impossible. "'Go' sayith the Lord, 'and sin no more!'"

I asked my teacher, "What is a sin?"

"You don't have to worry about that now," she said.

I was baptized on my eight birthday, wearing a white gauze dress and dunked under water in a big bathtub, washing away *all* my sins. Now sins, whatever they be, would be on my permanent record. Somehow, Jesus and God the Father knew my every move. I reasoned he was *sorta* like Santa, only God was fierce. If I were a bad little girl, Santa wouldn't bring presents; however, if I were bad in God's eyes, I wouldn't go to Heaven. The only love I had to compare to God's love was the love of my parents and sisters. They were *My* Gods. They loved me and didn't have conditions.

Confliction with my faith bothered me throughout childhood and into young adulthood. I hated church and stopped going though still feeling the need for salvation. Years passed before guilt led me to the *Fast and Testimony Meeting*, held the first Sunday every month. The faithful bear verbal witness to the gospel of Jesus Christ, in front of the congregation. I still had a burning desire to save my two little children and myself. Therefore, we went. Nervous and full of apprehension, I watched the loyal followers march to the podium and bear their testimony. They'd survived the most horrific ordeals, which left me wondering if indeed, I wanted to be a member. I surmised the Lord gave devout followers a more potent set of problems. Regardless, I wanted to understand their unwavering faith. Why do they feel blessed and grateful despite their trials and tribulations? Why don't they hate the Lord and scream at Him for making their lives difficult? I concluded the Spirit of the Lord inspires one while standing before the congregation bearing witness. *Maybe I'll be infused with the Holy Ghost and enlightened if I give my testimony.*

Wearing pants to chapel that morning was also a test; I wanted to see if God would strike me dead for defiance. Swallowing hard, I eased out of the pew and headed to the pulpit. *Please Heavenly Father, move me, show me, and fill my heart!*

Feeling light as if I were floating out of my body and peering down from above, the faithful, whose faces expressed unknowing, watched me take the microphone. I stood frozen…words weren't coming. God didn't move my heart to speak like I'd hoped. *Shit, I shouldn't have worn pants. What was I thinking? I'm so embarrassed! I have to say something!* Quivering, I said, "I can't bear witness to God, I don't know if this is the one true church or if Jesus lives and is my savior. I don't know if Joseph Smith is a true profit of God." I started to cry, tears flowing, I confessed my only testimony of truth, "All I know is *I love my parents!*" Silence fell over the congregation and there were a few gasps. People whispered as I returned to the pew where my children sat. I bent down and with a calm voice said, "Kids, come with me." That morning I put my relationship with the Lord on the back burner and looked for justification to make not attending church acceptable.

As a child, our family's church was an old adobe building surrounded by feed stores and horse corrals. Inside, the chapel was cool, dark and gloomy, and the only light streamed from colorful glass windows. A multi-colored circular, stained glass window centered high in the rafters above the organ, depicted an angelic looking man with shoulder length brown hair, his eyes cast upward, on his knees, praying. Having never seen a picture of God, I assumed it was Jesus. I thought, *Jesus looks nice, but his dad seems mean. God is always angry about something! God is supposed to be my father in Heaven; I like my daddy on earth.*

Upon entering church Sunday morning, the air smelled like stale 'morning mouth' and got worse as the congregation sang, "Welcome, Welcome, Sabbath Morning." Then after the opening service, we took the sacrament, the Mormon equivalent to the Catholic Eucharist. Instead of wine, we were given water and a smooched up piece of white bread the young Deacons tore into little pieces with their grimy fingers. *Jesus died for our sins. How does that work? Because we are bad, God's kid has to die.* It scared me; consequently, I was terrified of God. After my baptism, I learned about the three degrees of glory: Celestial, Terrestrial, and Telestial Kingdoms. I was told they were the ultimate eternal dwelling places for nearly all who've lived on earth. Mormon heaven isn't one gigantic place where all souls live out eternity in a state of bliss. Depending on how you live on earth, when you die, you live out eternity in one of these kingdoms. Mormons don't believe in Hell, per say. The few who do not inherit a *degree of glory* reside in *Outer Darkness*, also known as *Sons of Perdition*. The Big Kahuna is the Celestial Kingdom. I was sure everyone in the family would go to the "CK" and I wasn't about to do anything to screw that up. Secretly, I thought it reduced God to a spiritual game show host. "Behind each door is a kingdom. Listen carefully, and you will hear three versions of the Truth. There is only one *right* Truth. If you pick the *right* Truth, you will live eternity in the fabulous...dum, da da, dum...Celestial Kingdom. But, if you choose the *wrong* Truth, you will be sent to a lesser Kingdom for eternity, or, God forbid, *Outer Darkness!*"

God must be an idiot. Did the Creator of everything really design such a complicated plan?

Mother and Daddy met at Brigham Young University and married *for time and all eternity* in the Mormon Temple in Salt Lake City, Utah. Their love was a major influence on my life and from them I modeled the kind of relationship I wanted. When I was young, I believed someday I would find a man and live happily ever after as they have for 67 years—an ever growing love story.

"Girls, let's go, your father is on his way home and I want to be there," she'd say. We felt his homecoming was a special event, which usually consisted of a romantic smooch and Daddy saying, "Your mother is the cutest girl in town—Oh, I love this girl." These small lovely gestures imprinted on my psyche, leading me to believe marriage was special and wonderful, and all parents were like mine. My childhood was carefree and magical. Our family was close; we enjoyed each other, played together, talked openly, and weren't hesitant to display affection with hugs and kisses. We knew we were loved. I remember in high school talking freely about most subjects; we had few rules and no curfew. We understood sex before marriage—a no, no.

"Endure to the end," a mantra I heard often from other church-goers, reminding us our life is not easy here on earth; however, eternity will be worth all this enduring, if we kept the Lords commandments. I had no reason to believe life wouldn't always be a fairytale when I was a kid. As I matured, the facade started to crumble; I wasn't prepared for the harsh realities of life. My sheltering left me with a lot to figure out. The church continued fueling my skepticism. *Why would I have to marry a Mormon or convert a non-Mormon into the Celestial Kingdom?*

In junior high, my sister Carol and I attended a church service during a family trip to Salt Lake. After the sacrament, we attended a Sunday school class taught by Sister Harrington; she began with, "Do you know how special you are belonging to the *one true church*?" There are people, for instance, who are Catholic, and don't know the Truth." Amazed by her condemnation, Carol and I rolled our eyes. I whispered to Carol, "What if I tell her we're not Mormons?"

"Yes, dear? I don't believe I recognize you," she said.

"We're from Tucson, Arizona. I'm Gloria and she's my sister Carol. Our friends back home suggested we visit your church. However, we're Catholic. Is it okay to be here?"

"Oh, yes, were happy you're here," she said looking embarrassed and with an insincere grin. "Will you be returning next Sunday?"

Carol and I elbowed each other, barely able to hold back howls and, as soon as the class ended, quickly exited arm in arm. "I really zinged her, didn't I? I hope she learned her lesson." *Proud, I'd stood up to her.* When I began to explore the world on my own, happiness seemed harder to attain. There were disappointments: Not making the tennis team or becoming a cheerleader, and even more frustrating, I didn't make good grades. I truly wanted an uncomplicated, simple life, the way it was when I was a child. I came from a world of *being* and stepped into a world of conflict...I thought happiness was something outside myself I would have to attain. During my sophomore year, happiness was a guy named Harry Lodge.

Carol is two years older and we share a bedroom; she's my best friend and mentor. I confided that I had my eye on Harry and needed her advice. "You mean the guy who's the quarterback? Geez, Gloie, all the girls want to go out with him."

"Yeah, so what?"

"He's already got a girlfriend."

"I don't care; I really like him. He's so cute, I'm goin' for him."

Harry was a big man on campus, a junior, with chestnut hair, muscles and a great smile with a space between his two front teeth. He acted cocky swaggering down the hall wearing his Palo Verde High letterman's jacket with all the pins and stripes. It never occurred to me I wouldn't 'snag' him. I'd scheme to show up where he'd be hanging out. One day I deliberately bumped into him: "Gosh, we seem to keep running into each other, I'm Gloria. Are you new?"

"I'm Harry Lodge, the quarterback."

"Oops, I'm sorry; I didn't recognize you," I said, acting coy.

After that, I planned every encounter—I'd ask him for a ride, borrow a dollar 'cause I forgot my lunch money, anything to get in his face. By the time summer came, we had a date. When he picked me up, he made an outstanding impression on my parents. We *Hansen* girls had a reputation—our dad was famous for his 'date interrogations'. Harry played it right, asking Dad a million questions and flirting with Mom and my little sister, Peggy. They fell in love with him, and gave him their stamp of approval, which was essential. I was astounded since he wasn't a Mormon. By the time school started in the fall, we were an item. At Christmas, he gave me a diamond and pearl promise ring, and I believed we'd be together forever.

Carol returned home for summer break after her first year at the University of Utah. She told me, "I drink now!" If our parents knew, she wouldn't have gone back to U of U. That same summer, our family took a dream vacation to the first Club Med in Tahiti. Carol and I acted so grown-up, drinking red wine every evening from carafes put on the dining tables. Nonchalantly, we sneaked it into our bungalow and got soused.

Harry was now a senior, and one night after a football game, said, "You're not like the other girls I've dated. They're easy."

I was a good girl, a virgin and planned to stay one. God forbid I have sex before marriage, I would be condemned to *Outer Darkness* or one of the lesser kingdoms and my children wouldn't be sealed to me *for time and all eternity*! Sealing in the Temple meant our family would be together forever and ever, and I wasn't about to jeopardized that! Because Harry wasn't Mormon, I devised a plan to convert him, then re-marry him in the Temple, and all our butts would be saved. One night Harry and I steamed up the windows of his refurbished '57 Chevy, lots of heavy petting, grabbing my boobies, French kissing, everything but screwing. Then suddenly, he pushed me away and said, "I can't do this."

"What?" I couldn't believe he'd said that or pushed me away.

"I can't do this, I want sex, I need it."

"Harry, you know I can't!"

"Either you have sex with me, or I'll find someone who will! I love you; don't you love me?" he cajoled.

For six months, I dreamed of going to my Junior Prom with him; we would walk in arm-in-arm, everyone would know we were in love. My imagination was perfect. However, that disappeared when he called all excited and announced, "Glo, my parents are going out of town."

"When?"

"Prom weekend."

"What? Where are they going?" I asked, dismayed by his excitement.

"Who cares, it doesn't matter. What's wrong with you? You sound hesitant. You know Glo, you said…"

"I know, I know what I said, but *prom* night?" *Why did I promise?*

"This could be our only chance. You promised, Glo." he pressed.

Prom day I primped and acted eager while getting ready; no one suspected anything unusual. I knew the deception and felt nauseated. After posing for photos, we left my unsuspecting parents and headed to his empty house. It was dark and smelled like cigarettes. He grabbed my hand and led me down the hall to his bedroom; my heart was as dark as the house. *How can I do this, why did I promise? I do love him and want to please him, but this is happening too fast.* Like a robot following orders, I agreed to the unspeakable. He flipped on the light; his room was small, almost consumed by the double bed, and thumb tacked to corkboard walls—colorful little league banners. While caressing the soft, velvety yellow rose– only minutes before pinned to my chiffon gown–I hesitated, and hated myself for what I was about to do. I laid the pearl tipped pin and rose gently on the bedside table. *What have I done?* "Please, turn out the light Harry." He grinned and tried to convince me everything would be okay, but he stood there looking down at his *'stiffy'*. I'd never seen a naked man and I wasn't sure I liked what I saw. He didn't say anything else, just grunted and moaned. He didn't say I was beautiful or that he loved me and I would always be his girl. *It's not supposed to be like this. I want to be a virgin and married for time and all eternity in the Temple. Why did Mama tell me sex was fun and special and I'd enjoy it?* With every thrust, the wooden headboard banged against the wall. I equated my plight to Jesus' being nailed to the cross and wondered how I could put myself back together and pretend all was well. *My beautiful hairdo is a mess…when will he finish? Yuk, this hurts, he smells like sweat and Old Spice – I want him off! Is this what I have to do to keep you?* Then, suddenly he gasped and pulled out. White gooey stuff spewed on my tummy.

"Harry, what is that? Wipe it off! Hurry!"

He jumped up and ran to the bathroom; I could hear him throwing up. *Did I do something wrong, or make him sick?* Fear overcame me! I'd sinned and closed the door on any other choice. *I'll have to marry him. Then surely, God will forgive me, but will he?* I lost my self-respect, I was a liar, and my optimism about life became blurred. I no longer trusted Harry and my love for him became tainted. *I'm one of those easy girls now and probably condemned to Outer Darkness.* Worrying about the consequences of our forbidden act became a burden and worsened every time we had sex, becoming more and more impossible to bear. I stuffed my feelings and pretended I was a good girl, but deep inside I felt dirty, ashamed and immoral. I told no one, not even my loving, understanding family. My sinful choice was my fall from Grace, which changed my life. I ignored my core beliefs and values, and thus began my downward spiral.

Harry and I were together thirteen years. We married four years after our first date and had two beautiful children. Funny, though not at the time, and thinking about it now, we never used birth control, and every month I was afraid I could be pregnant. I regret not dating other guys, kissing other boys, a lot more boys. I wish I'd experienced more on my own, had bigger dreams and goals. My future was set, or I believed it was, and only until much later did I realize the choices I made were all mine. I've wasted a lot of life chasing happiness, expecting someone to give it to me, show it to me, and buy it for me. I was always anxious, waiting for something better and who knows what to happen.

Except for the Club Med vacation, I didn't drink until Harry joined the Fijis, a fraternity at the University of Arizona. I was a senior in high school and thought I was big stuff–going to wild college parties, drinking and casting aside inhibitions, certainly not living the gospel. After our marriage, I became disillusioned and the clichéd *Seven Year Itch* took over. Booze made life bearable. Before long, binging at parties escalated to afternoon pick-me-ups. I drank to unwind while making dinner, and more to fall asleep. It came full circle when I needed a nip to face the day. I lost track of how much I was drinking, when the line between morning and night became skewed. Harry and I no longer made love; I felt more alone with him than not, and hated sleeping in the same bed, so I drank more. I thought having a boob job would put spark back into our marriage, and that failed. Then I remembered how alive I felt when I met Bob, the guy Harry introduced at the business party. Our clandestine rendezvous was the demise of my nine-year-marriage. Bob was like a drug, and I didn't care who I hurt. All I wanted was him inside me filling in the emptiness. No one knew the battle that raged inside me. My parents considered Harry their son, and thus I believed they wouldn't understand my unhappiness; I had everything. While visiting Mother, she accused me of having an affair. Her words almost knocked me out: *how did she know?*

"Gloria, you're sleeping with someone aren't you? What's the matter with you? You have a family and adoring husband. How could you do such a thing?"

"Please, let me bring Bob over, at least give him a chance," I begged. "I love him; I'm finally happy. I'm miserable with Harry."

When at last I was permitted to bring Bob to meet my family, it was short of halleluiah. I remember Bob's parting words, "Don't worry; you'll get used to me."

Later that day, Mama called. Her warning alarmed me, "If you leave town with that guy, you might as well take a gun to my head, Gloria!"

Well that was it. I filed for divorce and left Tucson hoping happiness was 100 miles north—Phoenix—Bob—new life—new love, fulfillment within reach. Again, happiness was somewhere out there, and I had to find it! Poor Bob, he could hardly afford living, let alone have an instant family with a dog, cat and lover with an addiction to pills and booze. The only neighborhood we could afford had no vegetation—devoid of bushes and trees—bleak and tan. Furthermore, I had no friends. Someone alerted the LDS brethren and soon they came calling. Disgusted by their proselytizing, I fell deeper into booze and my fear and hatred of God more intense. Mornings, I pounded down *Wild Turkey* and would sober up enough by afternoon to pick the kids up from school. I couldn't believe it when Harry told me he wanted custody of the children and would hire an attorney to get them. I was so out of it, I actually considered it might be easier to let him have them. However, when I asked Bob, he paused and said, "I'm afraid you'd regret it the rest of your life."

I had committed every egregious sin against God: premarital sex, alcoholic, adulterer, not living the gospel, and now considering giving my kids away! I felt worthless, and life had become as they say in AA, unmanageable. I thought suicide could stop the pain; I planned taking an overdose or driving off a cliff. But, whenever I thought about my kids, parents, sisters, and how killing myself would devastate them, coupled with God and his wrath… I overruled that idea.

I'll never forget the night Bob came home and found me cowering in the closet, drunk and disoriented. "Gloria, I love you, but I won't live with a drunk. It's not my job to make you happy!" I couldn't believe what he was saying, *if it's not his job, then why the hell did I move to Phoenix?*

I had to do something, but hesitated, and then I decided to go to an Alcoholics Anonymous meeting. *Shit, these people are weird, I'm not like them.* Through sheer determination, I managed to stop drinking and convinced everyone I was sober. After three years of marriage and twelve months of sobriety, Bob and I decided to have a baby. We named our precious and perfect girl Taylor. I had been clean throughout my pregnancy, and reasoned if I could go twelve months, I wasn't an alcoholic, and set out to prove it. While fixing dinner one evening, I decided to have a glass of wine. The nightmare returned. I kept telling myself, *I can control this thing, I'm not an alcoholic.*

One afternoon the phone rang, "Hi Glo", Daddy's happy voice. "Hey, Allyn and I are stopped for gas nearby on our way to Flagstaff, Kelly's car broke down and we thought since we're so close, it would be nice to see you. Can we drop by?" Allyn's my older sister and Kelly's her son. When they arrived, I was drunk. Opening the front door, Daddy took one look at me and his smile turned to devastation. His broken heart—acid to my soul, I finally hit rock bottom!

There was no equivocation. I had to quit. The decision was mine, and I chose to control, rather than be controlled. With each new day, I became clearer; fear and shame moved out, I had no more excuses. Besides, I was weary of lying and blaming everyone else for my misery. If I didn't change, I would lose everything I held near and loved. Seventeen years of torturing myself for what? Something clicked, and I knew deep inside, I would never be controlled by guilt, drugs or alcohol again. *How could a little girl from Utah, born into love, sheltered and adored have fallen so deep into darkness?* My fall from Grace Prom night set me on a path of self-destruction. Guilt and fear poisoned my spirit. I had no way of knowing pain was my Savior delivering answers through re-birthing—walking Hell's fire, drenched in booze and vomit, a pain so excruciating, death looked sweet. I had to get out of darkness…push, push, push—light, love, air, within reach outside this torturous womb.

Allyn sent a letter and enclosed a poem she thought might give me strength. Ironically, it was the very poem a man at the AA meeting I'd attended the night before was trying to remember. It's called "Act as If." It was the affirmation I needed, and realized there was something greater than me at work. I've never gone back to AA. For me I had to regain my inner power that I'd given away. Alcohol deadened the loss. The beautiful mystery of self-discovery and learning the answers to my provocative questions are better than anything imaginable. No longer myopic, I could see where my fall from Grace led me to taking those first new steps after years of only knowing how to crawl. In retrospect, I've always been safe and home; my salvation was never in jeopardy. I did not find my truth through religion, fear or superstition. I found it through the love I received at birth. I hadn't been forsaken. The answers and love had always been there, waiting for me; sweet, precious love with no conditions.

Shortly after my awakening, I got a fortune cookie, it read, "We are living in an eternity, the time to be happy is now!"

Prom 'dos!
Me and my sister

Smooch!

Tahiti-bound!
Peggy, Mom, Glo, and Carol

Epilogue

"Sure, I'll be in your book." My response when Mary presented this opportunity. She said we needed to write 30 to 60 pages, and read a selection from it during our Santa Fe get together in September. It sounded easy; however, I'd never met any of these women. Reality set in while sitting at my computer waiting for words to appear. "Shoot, I can't write, certainly not for people I don't know. Crap, what about me will be interesting?"

The deadline was fast approaching, and every day I felt tortured. I worked harder at not doing than doing. It's my greatest fear, the dream that keeps repeating...*I'm in high school, and it's test day, I forgot to study and can't remember the combination to my locker, and I'm nude!*

I wrote a great email to Mary explaining it would be impossible for me to fit this into my busy schedule. "Sorry, to let you down, thanks for including me, I wish you all the best..." pressed send and took a nap, "Whew; I fixed that problem, now I can relax."

When I awoke, Mary had written back. "You're not letting me down, you're letting *yourself* down!" That was one swift kick in the butt, but it started me going, and has been a grand experience. I've learned things about myself that were hidden and locked away; things I thought I wanted locked away. *The truth shall set you free*, is the Truth! I am born again, stronger, lighter, and happier than ever. Clarity and forgiveness of self is a wonderful gift.

Writing my story has opened me to knowing myself in ways I never knew. The second half of my life is dedicated to healing, forgiving past hurts and living with peace of heart. Sharing my darkest, deepest, hidden story with my wonderful new sister friends, and listening to their stories, has reminded me we are all walking wounded, products of our experiences.

I would encourage everyone to write his or her life story. Dig deep, put in the details, and *remember!* I believe peace is an inside job–don't expect someone else to save you or save our world. You are captain of your vessel. Start first with you, and you'll see when you are serene, it's infectious; people are drawn to your light. We need to be gentle with each other. The madness and insanity ends when each of us end it.

Gloria Hansen Morrison

Gloria

Jill Stouffer

I'm joyful leaving insecurities behind, and looking forward to an exciting new chapter in life. I packed my potential and all I've learned in life's suitcase and bid farewell to my forties. I walked into the sandwich shop–now caught between raising two teenage sons and care-giving my aging mother who has debilitating Rheumatoid arthritis and early signs of dementia.

I wonder how this happened to me.

From childhood, weight and lack of confidence were constant battles. I'm a late bloomer, and truly I thank god for recognizing this, and I intend to flourish the remainder of my life. My husband and I have been married twenty years and were in our thirties when our children we born.

I have a bachelor's degree from the University of Arizona and work in our family glass business. We live in Scottsdale, Arizona.

Rear View Mirror

By

Jill Stouffer

Life begins at the end of your comfort zone.
- **Neal Donald Walsch**

The IV drip and heart monitor are the only sounds in the room. I'm sad, and grieving the loss of vitality for the once thriving, capable and self-sufficient woman lying motionless before me. Gripping the rail of Mom's hospital bed, I want this to go away, stop. At the same time, my parallel brain jolts me into reality. A faraway voice whispers, *"This isn't going away, Jill." Thank god, she's asleep and can't see into my eyes; she always knows what I'm thinking. I can't bear to see you like this Mom. Shit, where are Pam and Tracy? I'm sick of taking care of these things myself. I've picked up the pieces for so long now, everyone expects me to. Besides, I'm tired and have my own family; my kids and Jim need me. Shit, I need me. The magnitude of this is overwhelming, I can't do it, won't do it, not again. Oh, my god, did I say all that out loud?*

Glancing over my shoulder, I'm relieved to see the nurse is down the hall. Just then, the doctor, nonchalant and confident, saunters into the room and says, "I wouldn't worry too much about your mother; she's out of danger, but there is a possibility that she won't be able to care for herself. Are you prepared to take care of her? If not, does she have the means to hire someone?"

I shrug my shoulders and shake my head, not knowing how to respond. My mind is fuzzy, and my stomach had an empty ache. *What if she has to stay with us for good? I don't think I can do it. I'll kiss her goodbye, leave the hospital, and run away from this nightmare.*

Where are my fucking keys? Digging around inside my purse is futile. *Crap, I don't remember sticking them in my pocket; I never put things in my pockets.*

Leaving her room and the medicinal smell of the hospital for the sanctuary of my car, I scream, "This can't be happening!" I cry until I can cry no more, and my head is throbbing. Looking into the rear view mirror as I pull out of the parking space, I see beady, red pig eyes staring back. Driving up Scottsdale Road, my BMW feels like a parachute; quiet, safe, peaceful. Alone, I glide onto the interstate. Halfway home the freeway splits, and I'm tempted to take the exit north, the same escape route I'd taken years before when Bill, my first love, left.

Sensibility overrides irrationality. In a few minutes, the garage door opens, and the familiar signs of a family with boys: ATV's, dirt bikes, basketballs and hockey sticks strewn about. For a nanosecond, I think of backing out, hitting the gas and leaving. The steering wheel props my weary arms and head; my body is drained and paralyzed. Jim opens the kitchen door and says, "Jill, are you okay?"

Getting out of the car, I snap, "I told you before we were married, I wasn't a care giver, and if it ever came to this, I couldn't do it."

"Do what? What are you talking about?" he asks, then smiles his *grab my heart* smile, laughs, and says, "Come inside."

"God dammit, this is no laughing matter. I can't take care of my mother! How can I feel like this? She's my mother! She was my life, my strength, and now I'm pissed at her for getting sick. Furthermore, I'm left with the responsibility of caring for her. And to top it off, I feel horrible, guilty and ashamed."

"Jill, you're tired, why don't you take a warm bath and go to bed? I'm sure you'll feel better tomorrow."

I'm lying in bed, exhausted and needing sleep, but staring at the ceiling. *It's uncommon for Jim to rustle about in bed, is he worried too?* My mind slips back to childhood and fourth grade. Dad and I were standing in the kitchen of our Tucson home. I remember him saying, "Jill, you better stop drinking so much orange juice. It's full of sugar, and you don't want to end up getting fat and looking like Aunt Jane Ann." Aunt Jane Ann was obese. Her arms jiggled, and her stomach hung below her crotch. When she sat at the dining table, blobs of fat oozed over the sides of the chair.

"I'm not going to look like her." *How could he think that?* The minute he backed our white *Buick* out of the carport on his way to work, I thought, *I'll show him*, and raced to the refrigerator, grabbed the bottle of OJ and chugged down the last drop. Burping, and feeling whole again, I headed out the door to my girlfriend Theresa's house.

Little did he know I saved my lunch money to buy *Sweet Tarts* after school. I didn't eat lunch because I'd rather wait for the little candy that tasted so good and made my mouth pucker. The name said it all — the cherry, lemon and lime flavors burst into granules in the roof of my mouth. The sad truth was my overeating and indulgences began to show in a not-so-little way on my body.

His remarks were painful. *I wonder if he knew what they did to me.* Mom would never say anything so awful to me. Her love was and has always been unconditional. However, Dad was very careful never to say those things in front of her. She would have been furious. Mom worked full-time as a teacher and took night classes to earn her Master's Degree. *I knew she wanted more for herself and our family.*

Theresa wore her hair in a ponytail, and I decided I'd wear mine that way too. One day Dad said, "Jill, why are you wearing your hair pulled behind your ears?"

"What's wrong with me wearing a ponytail, Dad?"

"Well, you look better when you wear your hair down because your ears stick out." I was embarrassed and turned bright red as tears welled. I ran to the bathroom and pulled long strands from the rubber band, releasing dark brown curtains of hair to cover my gigantic ears. Never again would I wear a ponytail in front of him, and from that time on, I wore it straight and parted down the middle.

Theresa's family was different; her dad never said unkind things to her. I was accepted there and liked going to their house. I remember hearing her dad tell her he loved her; I wished Dad could tell me he loves me. Her dad complimented her too, "Theresa, you did a great job cleaning the back porch." I did all sorts of chores at home without any thanks or compliments from my Dad. A time came when I built the courage to ask him if he loved me. I was somewhat sure of his answer, which would be a half-hearted uh-huh. I wasn't cute and skinny like my little sister, Tracy. Besides, Mom mentioned he wanted to have a son and planned on naming him Jack…not Jill. Finally, in eighth grade I summoned the courage to ask. He was sitting by the window in his recliner and reading the paper. I cleared my throat. He peeked over the paper and pulled his glasses down on his nose and said, "Do you want something, Jill?"

"Uh, Dad, do you love me?" I said, in an anticipatory voice. Lowering the paper to his lap and looking aggravated, he said, "Of course I do."

"Why can't you just say it to me, without my asking? I want to hear you say it."

"You know I love you, Jill. Don't be ridiculous! I don't want to talk about this anymore."

Now twenty years later, I'm sitting in my father's tiny apartment. My parents are divorced and he's suffering with terminal lung cancer. Every weekend I drive a hundred miles to be with him. Driving gives me time to think about the life we lived in our little house on 24th Street, before I grew up and this happened. *I yearned for his validation, which never came.* I knock and open the door; there he is, sitting in the same place waiting for me. I rest my hands on his boney shoulders; his body feels rigid and shriveled. Cancer is shrinking him into a small man, not the big man I always thought he was when I was a kid. He has a tube with two prongs inserted into his nose, which spews oxygen keeping him alive. I'm revolted by his hacking and spitting into a bowl on the table. Our conversation begins with, "Jill, will you help me sort through these papers?" He pulled a box from under the table and shoved it toward me with his foot.

"Sure Dad, what are they?" *Is this half-full accordion file all he has?*

"It's legal stuff and insurance papers," he says, and starts to cry. Then from nowhere and not looking at me he said, "I love you, Jill. Will you be here next weekend?" When I was ready to leave, I kissed him on the cheek, and whispered, "I'll be here."

Driving back to Scottsdale rage begins to rise; my neck stiffens and I clinch the steering wheel, shouting, "Why is he telling me he loves me now?" *Ulterior motive, he always has a reason for everything. Ah, he's needy and wants me to come every weekend. Egad, why am I thinking this way? I'm not a vengeful person, but I have a hard time trusting his sincerity. Look what's happened to us. If only he'd told me he loved me when I so desperately needed to hear it, would things be different? Damn, I'm thirsty; I'd love to have a tall glass of cold, fresh squeezed orange juice.*

Between 6th and 7th grade, I gained ten pounds and it showed. The mirror doesn't lie. When I began noticing, my heart sank. I felt unattractive and worthless. I'd dreamed of trying out for cheerleading; however, my insecurities must have been obvious to the coach and she rejected me after try-outs. During lunch-break, I yearned to sit at the table with the eight most popular girls in school; they were slim, tall and to my surprise, ate *Gerber's* baby food — strained bananas. *That must be how they stay skinny. I'd rather have a Long John with maple frosting.*

By the time I started high school, I'd tried the grapefruit diet, low-carb diet, and not eating altogether. The thin girls were the ones the athletes dated. I equated thin with perfection, something I wasn't. Overweight, depressed, self-conscious and with a negative attitude, I decided I was sick, had a disease. The only place I felt wanted was while babysitting. Our neighbors wanted me every weekend, and started booking weeks in advance. I also helped take care of my little sisters. I had very little extra time to do anything else–no sleepovers with friends, or even shopping. Looking back now and understanding how any number of these situations may have contributed to my lack of confidence, it's no wonder I ended up weighing 200 pounds.

At fifteen, I lied about my age to get a job at *Dunkin'Donuts*. It was a real job, *not just babysitting.* I was twenty pounds overweight and working in a doughnut shop. Wearing the traditional rosy-pink uniform, I felt cute. One day, the place was hopping, full of customers lined up waiting to order. I noticed a greasy haired, smarmy looking guy sitting at the end of the counter. I guess he was in his early 30s. While I watched, he tore the doughnut into quarters with his grimy hands and laid each piece side by side on the counter top. Then, one-by-one, he dunked them into his coffee and finished by slurping down the last drop and running his tongue around his lips, licking off the remaining particles. "Ahhh", he said, then winked and waved his hand motioning me to come over. I grabbed the coffee pot assuming he wanted a refill.

"Honey, I just want to tell you…you're the prettiest girl I know."

Honey, I don't think anyone has called me that before, I kinda like it.

He had a mischievous grin from ear-to-ear on his cocked head, and went on to say, "All the rest are tied for first." I was stunned and held on to the edge of the counter for support. I can't believe he said that. I don't remember much after, but somehow I managed to get to the back room before tears exploded. My boss looked worried and asked if I was alright. I told him I was ill and needed to go home.

"Sure Jill, no problem. Here, take a box of fresh double stuffed to your family," he said. I called Mom under the pretense we weren't busy, and asked if she could pick me up. When she came, I didn't share my devastation with her. How could I tell her what that horrible man said– *she had the ugliest daughter in the world?* As it turned out, the box of Boston creams tucked under my arm ended up in my room, and I consumed every crumb…stuffing my pain and filling the void inside, I swallowed my pride with every damn bite. I bought into the nasty man's insinuation. *I am the ugliest girl in the world.* The sad part is I defined myself by his venomous comment for years.

Before college, I lost weight and gained control of my over-eating. I went on dates, pledged Alpha Delta Pi, worked out and bought new clothes. The thrill unequal to anything I'd experienced before: *guys found me attractive.* I met Bill and we were inseparable; I planned our life together, he was my fantasy come to life. His bronze skin, light blue eyes and sun streaked blonde hair: a vision—he was beautiful, and all mine. However, our two years together were one-sided. He met someone else and—blotto, I was out. He said I was negative and down on myself, and he didn't want to be around that energy. Now all the years of self-criticism and doubt flooded over me again, validating—undesirable. I didn't return to school that semester. Instead, I headed north, driving my 1976 yellow *Datsun B-210, Honey Bee*; windows down, eight-track blaring *The Eagles' "Tequila Sunrise"* over and over. Going north, I ate my way through Flagstaff and stops along the way, ending up at a friend's house in Colorado, where food became my lover. I returned home for the holidays wearing overalls and hiding my shame—having fulfilled Dad's prophecy. *Oh my god, I <u>am</u> Aunt Jane Ann.*

I went back to school and completed my degree at the University of Arizona. I moved to Phoenix eager to start a new life. The growing metro was exciting and there were opportunities galore. In no time, I got a job with a financial planning firm. I was the only woman, surrounded by cordial and respectful men. My confidence grew, and I saw a brighter future. I began jogging and running 5Ks. I threw away my bulky gray sweats and replaced them with cute running shorts and bra tops in coordinating bold colors. My journey of self-discovery began.

Feeling empowered gave me courage to find an even better paying job. Peter, my new boss, told me how much he appreciated my work and encouraged me to think about my future and potential with the company. He was a positive role model; truthfully, I considered him a father figure. I even fantasized he might walk me down the aisle someday and give my hand to a wonderful man.

The Christmas holiday arrived and–while I was leaving the building—*he* was coming in. I was almost out the door when I overheard Tom, a guy from another office whisper, "That's her." *Was he referring to me?* Once inside my car, I thought about the guy I caught a glimpse of—*did we, or did we not lock eyes?* During the holidays, my mind wandered to the man with the dark curls, olive skin, and sparkling green eyes with the infectious smile. The New Year came, and it was back to work. However, it wasn't long before Tom and his wife invited me to dinner and admitted they were going to introduce me to Jim. *So, that's his name.* We hit it off and began dating. He told me I was smart, funny and gorgeous. Soon we were inseparable. Our childhood experiences were similar—he was the oldest of three children, as was I. We went on trips to the beach and to wine country. We *fit*. My insecurities melted away with him. We bought a house and moved in together. Jim proposed marriage, and said he wanted me to be the mother of his children, and if we had a son, he wanted to name him Tanner. Baby Tanner was born three years after our wedding and son Carter followed fifteen months after Tanner. We had a beautiful family—all I'd ever wanted.

Eighteen years have passed and while I sit in the comfort of my home in Scottsdale, dread washes over me. I never imagined this moment…Mom, who has been my rock, and source of strength, sits scrunched like a child in our rust oversized club chair. Her nurses and care manager left a few minutes ago. Their parting words to me: "You'll get the hang of changing the 'bag' in no time, and everything will be fine." I wasn't buying it. Mom had a bowel obstruction, brought on from the painkillers she took following surgery for elbow replacement. I rushed her to the hospital, and thank god, the doctors saved her, but she ended up having a colostomy. She's almost unrecognizable and my frustration is evident when Ossa, her in-home nurse, asked me to sit down so he can help me. *Shit, where are my sisters?* I know where they are; Pam lives on the east coast with her son, and Tracy is close by but not able to help. Still, I was agitated; I was the one with the burden of her care. "Ma'am, everyone starts out feeling the same as you," he said. "I'll be here helping you." Even when Mom's insurance ran out, he continued coming. *Is he an angel?* My patience was running out; her insensitivity to my exhaustion irritated me more. I didn't have time for my husband, kids or myself. When I woke up in the morning, I squeezed my eyes shut again and clinched my fists, knowing I have another day of making her breakfast, helping her shower, getting her dressed, then changing the god damn bag and listening to her silly comments about the undigested food in it–made me want to scream.

"Aha, there's a raisin," she says, laughing.

"Mom, please don't say that. I'm aware of everything you eat."

"Well, there it is–look right there–one of the raisins from the bran muffin I ate yesterday."

Sometimes the bag stinks–reminiscent, but ten times worse than crappy diapers. *Stinky babies are acceptable, stinky mothers are not!*

One morning the clip slipped off the bag and shit splattered on Mom and me, then oozed down the front of her stomach and dripped on the bath mat. I screamed, "Jim!"

"I'm coming, I'm coming," he shouted, racing to the bathroom asking, "What?" He saw the mess, and my losing it… "Throw the fucking mat away!" I shrieked.

"Okay, calm down, I'll wash it off," he said softly.

"NO!" was all I said before collapsing on the floor. My hands covering my eyes, I sobbed uncontrollably, feeling as though my life was slipping through my fingers. He bent over and whispered, "Why don't you go clean up? I'll help your Mom."

The warm shower washed over my body, cleansing my heart and soul and removing remnants of her bran muffin. I put on sweats, threw my soiled clothes in the washer, and returned to the bathroom. There she sits on the toilet seat, wrapped in her plush light blue robe, her gray-blonde hair stringy wet, and Jim on his hands and knees cleaning up the mess.

Epiphany! — Mom's the one with shit coming out of the middle of her body.

Suddenly, I was shocked back to reality; this was the pivotal moment, forcing me to reevaluate my values and beliefs. It's up to me to make it okay for me. On some level deep inside my soul, I went beyond, and didn't even realize what happened. Almost as if a wand waved over my head—be calm, patient, and kinder my hostility toward her stilled; however, I must admit I can become overwhelmed, when I think about carrying every inch of responsibility for her life. Some of the credit has to be given to the new sealed, disposable, no-clip easy-to-use colostomy bags.

In hindsight, three months out of my life taking care of Mother in her time of need seems miniscule considering the brief amount of time it took her to recuperate and return home to Tucson where she is happy having her life back and I'm happy being back in mine.

Roles reversed, I'm blessed having time to care, protect, console, and shelter her. She knows time is slipping away, and too, her memory. Oftentimes, she doesn't remember what she did yesterday. She delights telling stories from her childhood, and I appreciate seeing her life through *her rear view mirror*. I listen and pay attention to her stories, no matter how repetitious they are, just as she did when I'd come blasting into the house, excited with great news having witnessed Theresa's dog Molly giving birth to ten puppies, and begging her to let us have one, just one: "Please, Mom, please."

Jill on the right Dunkin' Donuts pink?

Epilogue

I've arrived at a destination I hadn't charted, not realizing it would be a journey rich beyond my imagination, however, I continue to have numerous unanswered questions. Many emotions and feelings rose to the surface while writing; and I know how toxic and debilitating they have been throughout my life. Writing my story was a catharsis which aided me to bring to my conscious mind information about myself I've ignored, put away, hidden, stuffed and denied–both good and bad. All those things combined make up the real "Jill." Learning about me and accepting all of me will take time, and with help from a therapist, I'm on my way to better understanding why I reacted so overtly to things that eventually happen to everyone. I am becoming better equipped to handle whatever comes my way!

Jill Stouffer

Jill

Catherine Muldoon

I'm sixty-six, happy, and grateful to be alive. My husband Fred and I've been married thirty-six years; we currently live in New Jersey. We have two adult sons and a baby grandson. I was born in Missouri and moved to Arizona with my mother when I was eight. She was my inspiration–a dedicated and selfless registered nurse. By most standards, we were poor, and when I left home for college, my wardrobe consisted of a dress, a pair of shoes, a few blouses/tops and three pairs of jeans. I graduated from Arizona State University; work took me to Scotland and Mexico in the 70s. I traveled to many countries during my career working for Motorola and was among a very small group of women working for multinational companies at the time. I've taught both elementary and high school. I'm a passionate water-colorist and now, because of writing my story, I am passionate to write more. Fred and I are on the cusp of retirement, whatever that may be, and I look forward to an exciting future.

Message of the Gifts

By

Catherine Muldoon

Dark, uncertain, primeval thoughts emanate from those first minutes of regaining consciousness and my eyes detect an intense white light so blinding, I can't open them…!

Where am I?

As the dense fog lifts, a lighter more ethereal vapor pours into my head and some semi-rational thinking returns. A comforting sounding man reassures me saying, "Cathy, you're okay. We're almost done." Now awake, I see a tall man dressed in green scrubs and wearing a white surgical mask.

"We're putting the last sutures in your nasty cut; it's pretty deep and required about thirty stitches," he says.

"How could a snake bite do this?" I ask.

"What snake?" He asks bemused.

"The one in that box. It had to be a rattler!"

"We haven't had time to look inside the box," he says, glancing in the direction of the blood-soaked cardboard container, "But, I assure you it wasn't a snake. Your right hand will be sore and achy for about a week and you'll probably not be doing much writing, if any."

Shit, now I remember what happened and why I'm here…

On the drive home from the hospital, I began to laugh out loud remembering the other time I injured my poor right hand. "What's so funny?" Christy, my friend and driver asked. "Well, it was Memorial Day weekend 1970; I was home in Clarkdale visiting Mom and planning to clean out her garage for her belated Mother's Day present. She worked graveyard shift as a nurse supervisor at Marcus Lawrence Hospital, and has for years. When she wasn't sleeping during the day, she loved walking in the high desert, soaking in the fresh air and looking for ancient Native American potshards. I'd heard her well-meaning quips about the garage, but I know it is too difficult for her and perhaps injurious; so in lieu of flowers, I'd organize and clean her garage."

The corrugated iron garage door warped from years of harsh weather, making the metal loop-lock difficult to open. The second I touched the damn thing, I burned my right hand. I should have known better. The scorching Arizona sun had super-heated the lock, it felt like I'd grabbed onto a barbeque grill. It all started that weekend, and my good intentions of cleaning the garage changed my life in ways I'd never considered.

After treating the burn, I returned, determined to open the uncooperative hinged door. However, when I pull it, it flew open, causing me to stumble and land on my ass. Humiliated, I look to see if anyone saw what happened. All clear, so I went for the door one more time. Now that the friggin' thing was open, I saw the enormity of the task ahead. Years of cobwebs entomb the oily, greasy-smelling shed. The only light, a 60-watt bulb, hung from a cord tacked to a rafter. Somewhat regretting my offer, I'm reminded, *twenty-seven years she's selflessly supported me; this is the least I can do for her.*

Stuff is piled in grocery boxes filled mostly with *Reader's Digests*. Feeling exasperated and thinking I'd lost my mind taking this on alone, a shiny object catches my eye — it's the chrome on my blue *Schwinn*. Working my way over to the bike, I notice its flat tires and torn leather seat. It looks sad and aged. On the wall to the right of the door, a rusty saw, leaf rake, and shovel lean against Grandma's trunk. A compelling urge pulls me in that direction. Lifting off the top, I cringe at the stench. Clothes packed in mothballs since the early 1950s, along with her dingy, threadbare comforter are tucked tightly around everything — *looks like the mothballs didn't do their job*. Wool sweaters full of holes lay between her crocheted doilies and embroidered pillowcases with their lavender daisies lovingly stitched centers made of little orange French knots. I toss all the contents into an empty box and dig. There, as if awaiting discovery, a once elegant powder blue shirt box with scratched gold leaf lettering hid. Snatching it up, I carefully open it. Inside, yellowed envelopes addressed to Mom. Thumbing through the envelopes, it hits me. *Oh my god, these are love letters from my father to my mother during World War II.* Hesitant to investigate further and needing to get on with the job, I put the box aside. I zero in on a stack of magazines and old catalogs and grab the one on top. Blowing off the dust — a 1952 *Sears Christmas* catalog. A page with a bent corner marks where I'd circled in #2 pencil — skating doll.

"Make sure you pick out exactly what you want Santa to bring." I remember Mom saying.

Inside the dimly lit garage, tears fill my eyes. Now I understand the sacrifices she made as a single mother. Her legacy is a bank full of lessons learned, a lifetime of gifts that keep on giving. I hear her calling, "Cat, it's awful hot. Why don't you come inside and I'll fix you an iced tea?" I pick up the box and head toward the back door and to the kitchen, where she already sat the tea on my side of the table and waited. I put the box on the red and white checkered cloth. She looks at the box, then at me. "I found this in Grandma's trunk; do you know what's inside?" I ask, my heart pounding. "Uh, huh," she says in a matter-of-fact tone.

"Can I read them?"

"If you like."

Intruder, I am an intruder reading for-their-eyes-only tomes. "If we have a son, I want to name him David," he wrote. She responded, "If it's a girl, I want to call her Catherine, a name bestowed on girl babies each generation in my family."

She rose from the table and I watch her move around the kitchen, weaving back and forth from drying dishes to the cupboard. I try imagining them young and making love. I think she sensed my staring and turned around. "There's something else I want you to see. Come on, follow me to my room." I followed her to her bedroom and from underneath her bed, she pulled out an old, red, heart-shaped candy box and handed it to me—*how strange, after all this time, it still smells like chocolate.* It was full of pictures. Most were of her as a child, and one in particular made her laugh. *I loved hearing her laugh.*

"That's the day I graduated from nursing school. Can you believe that uniform?" She wasn't much younger than I am now, and her beauty was breathtaking. Then she handed me a stack of photos tied in black grosgrain ribbon.

"Who is this?" I ask.

"Your father," she replies in a soft voice.

He's striking, yet somehow familiar. Was I seeing me in him?

"What's this one?"

"That was taken on our wedding day in New Orleans."

"Wedding, really? Who was there?"

"No one, it was our special day, and besides ,his parents were not in favor because I was a Catholic and they were Jewish."

The 'who' in 'who am I' preoccupies my mind as I lay in bed later that night, trying to sleep. *I do have a father. Where is he? Should I try to find him?* Committing is easy, but where do I begin? I question a few of my friends and they recommend the library. As I enter the historic building, I approach the information desk. *How funny. She's everyone's idea of a librarian.* She is a 'wee tiny woman'; I picked up that expression while living in Scotland. Her wavy hair, wool dress, shoes, and rimmed glasses were all a shade of gray.

"I'm trying to locate my father, I know his name, date of birth and birthplace. Can you help me?"

"Possibly, let's take a look in the government directory."

The elevated black book filled the research desk; she flips through the pages with ease while I stand quietly behind, taking in everything. The morning sun streaming through the window, and the smell a mix of furniture wax and musty books, permeates the air.

Oak tables with those typical lamps and their green glass shades and worn leather chairs dot the room where four people sit engrossed. The only sound comes from pages flapping in the massive book.

"Here it is," she says. "The references are Social Security Administration, Bureau of Vital Statistics, and Veteran's Administration. They recommend writing a letter requesting information—here are the addresses." She smiles, and says, "I hope this helps."

I write and re-write the letters, when I finish, mail them, and breathe—relief. Two weeks pass, then three identical form letters came with instructions to send inquiries in an unsealed SASE. In bold it stated, **do not ask for money or make any threats!** Building enough courage to follow through kept the process going for three months. Each time I open the mailbox, I am gripped with anticipation, wanting and yet not wanting his letter. When it finally came, I couldn't open it. I tossed it on the coffee table and ignored it. Maybe that was some psychological payback for his years of ignoring me, or I was just plain afraid of what it might contain. Eventually, I carefully inserted the letter opener, slid out the paper and unfolded:

Dear Cathy,

Your letter came as a surprise to me and my family. I must admit, there have been many times I've wondered about you and if you knew about me. We live in Albuquerque, New Mexico. My wife Beverly and I have three teenage sons, Matt, Rob and Tim. I'm a retired Colonel, Army Corps of Engineers and now a civilian employee with the Corps working as a water-engineering specialist. Tell me about yourself; education—likes and dislikes—everything.

Waiting to hear from you,

Dad

I read and re-read; questioning feelings of doubt, but could not find the root. *He sounds nice, now what?* We corresponded for a year, most of it superficial, yak, yak, yak. Working for Motorola, I travel all over the world and am currently living in Guadalajara, Mexico. When I return home, a surprise awaits; Beverly invites me to visit sometime in October, the only time she says is open due to their very busy schedule with the boys' swim meets and extracurricular activities. *Do I really want to do this? Have I gotten so far into it, I can't back out?*

The flight from Phoenix to Albuquerque is short, and all I can think about is — *will I recognize him?* I'm anxious and my stomach growls. Getting off the plane I walk towards the exit and notice a short, chubby, gray- haired woman standing beside an adorable dark- haired boy. This unknown woman shouts, "Cathy, yoo-hoo! Cathy, we're over here."

How does she know who I am? Where is my father?

"Sorry, your father couldn't be here. He had to buy some wood; he'll join us at home."

I am disappointed he isn't there. *What sort of wood is more important?* Beverly and I chitchat in the car as we drive through an obviously middle class neighborhood, then pull into a carport of a house exemplifying the same status. Inside their meticulous home: displays of art and objects I recognize from all over the world. The two older boys seem happy to meet me, and likewise, me them. They are easy to talk with, *thank god*, saving me from Beverly. All of a sudden, the front door slams, interrupting our conversation. *He's here.* I hear footsteps racing down the hall and he bursts into the kitchen, sweeping me up in his arms, twirling about saying, "I have my little girl back, at last."

Did he actually say that? What is he doing?

"I have my little girl back, I have my little girl back," he repeats while Beverly stands off to the side looking disgusted by the scene. *Uh oh, that is not good!*

For the remainder of the afternoon, we went from room to room while he pointed out gifts from the South Korean government, photos of him with General Mac Arthur, President Eisenhower, and other notables. There were countless stories of testifying before Congress, and involvement in top-secret operations concerning our country's security. I didn't know whether to feel proud or exhausted. *What have I fallen into? This is surreal.*

My half-brothers were full of questions. Asking where I live, about my mom, school, other siblings, and where I grew up.

Since I'm a guest, I should offer to help Beverly prepare dinner. Upon entering the kitchen, she twirled around, glaring daggers, and said,

"I do not like sharing my men with another woman…and I won't!" Stunned, speechless and scared and wondering what just happened, she began barking orders, "Finish peeling these potatoes and set the table." My head was ready to burst and my heart raced. I tried remaining calm by sucking in the fury and biting my tongue. Dinner was agony, and at one point Tim asked why they hadn't visited me on their trip to Phoenix last Christmas. That was hush-hushed. *Hmm, how will Dad explain that?* Later that evening he brought it up saying, "You must be wondering what Tim meant about our trip to Phoenix?" I presume I looked quizzical; then he dropped the bomb, "We were there hiring a private investigator. Frankly, we thought you might be a fraud and there is money to consider."

What goddamn money? That's bullshit! How could he, a military man his entire life, now a retired Colonel, accrue money–especially, the kind of money he's insinuating I'm after?

Disgusted by what he'd said and appalled by his lack of sensitivity, had there been a way out, I would have left and never looked back. However, in my shy, non-confrontational, always-be-polite manner, I looked for the place of least difficulty — boys, family room, television. I lasted the two days, but not before Beverly took one more shot. In a snide tone she said, "Everything you see here will go to our sons. You may be his first born, but your father has three sons that require his attention now."

During the next couple of years, I visited them twice. Perhaps, I'd judged them too harshly, I'd give anyone else a second chance.

I was visiting and Dad suggested, "Let's take a ride, just the two of us. We'll go to one of my favorite places in the Sandia Mountains." He was right; I loved the fresh, crisp New Mexico air blowing in the window, bestowing kisses from mother earth. We made our way along a narrow red dirt road; conversation flowed easily and, for once, I felt comfortable. I finally mustered the courage to ask why he and Mom divorced. *God, what a huge mistake.* His entire demeanor changed. He swerved the car over to the shoulder and stopped. That's when he says, "My marriage to your mother is off limits. That's none of your business…end of conversation." *What the hell, I'm twenty-nine years old, have questions about my past he can answer, and he refuses!*

I returned home vowing not to subject myself to their crap again. However, the following spring my half-brother Rob is graduating from high school and I went back to Albuquerque.

Dad stood by the car, waiting for the entourage going to the ceremony. As I walked out the front door, he gazes at me as if in reverie, and says, "You look beautiful, exactly like your mother." Shrugging his shoulders, rolling his eyes, and acting as though he'd just stepped in dog shit was his reaction to Beverly's perturbation. *No doubt, she'll reward me for his faux pas.*

Winter 2010 was the most cantankerous, cold, and miserable I've experienced since living in New Jersey. Our plans were to be in Arizona, but the weather halted all travel. *In a few weeks I'll be sixty-six. How is that possible?* Watching ceaseless snow and ostracized indoors, I'm feeling blue about not going to Phoenix to share in my first grandchild's first Christmas. The continuum of flakes mesmerizes me. Resting my feet on the coffee table and sipping a hot cup of decaf Chai, thoughts regress, melancholy—Christmases.

I was twenty-eight when Dad's first gift landed on my doorstep. Giddy, like a child Christmas morning, I raced into the kitchen and grabbed a butcher knife to rip open the box. Failing in my excitement to turn on the light, and reaching into the shredded paper, eager to claim my gift, I shrieked. "Ouch, it bit me! Help!" My friend Christy, who'd dropped by, ran into the kitchen yelling, "Cathy, what's wrong?" Startled by the amount of blood on my clothes, table and gift box, she grabbed a dishtowel, wrapped my hand, picked up the box and said, "We're going to the ER."

I can laugh about it now, but at the time, it was serious and costly. My Stepmother made what I suppose she thought was an endearing gift; a red velvet bow with streamers, and glued on to the ribbons, jagged cat food can lids—a sort of mobile. When I reached inside the package, the sharp edge cut my right hand between my thumb and forefinger. I was sure a snake had bitten me. When the doctor kicked over the box and found the "Cat Mobile," everyone in the ER howled. That thoughtless fiasco landed me in the hospital and stuck me with a six-hundred-dollar bill that my insurance didn't cover. How she must have connived dreaming of retribution for Dad's misspoken "you look like your mother" remark. This was the first in a long line of Christmas gifts from Dad and his wife.

The following year, I returned from working in Scotland. Plans were made by friends I'd not seen in over a year to celebrate our reunion, share Christmas Eve dinner, and attend midnight mass. Around four p.m., a delivery: a package from New Orleans sent from Dad. Apparently, he'd been recalled to work on the levees. Not fearing what might be inside since it hadn't come from Beverly, I tore it open. Wadded up in newspaper, was a fake red lobster, and a note saying, "Wish this could be the real thing, Dad." *Was I missing something? Maybe I don't get his sense of humor, but a rubber, life-like lobster?*

Mass was about two hours and I returned home at 2:30 to find my precious dog Pippy not moving. Her breathing was labored, and she couldn't raise her head to show how happy she was to see me. Frantic to find a vet on Christmas morning, I called an emergency animal hospital and was told to get her there ASAP. The doctor whisked her out of my arms and disappeared. When he came back, he said she had ingested something toxic.

"Was there an ornament or something unusual in the house?"

"I don't think so."

"Regardless, she needs to stay here a couple of days on an IV to flush out the poison."

I felt horrible leaving her, and when I got home, I plopped down on the couch and scanned the room for something, anything out of place. "Ah ha" chunks of red, rubbery stuff lay hidden behind a wrapped present under the Christmas tree. Sick with guilt for not throwing the damn thing away—one more 'Dad-disaster'. *How many will there be?* Pippy recovered, thank heaven, but I was out a thousand dollars.

I yearned to meet someone; I missed having a relationship. Then I met Fred. I was back at Motorola in Phoenix awaiting my next assignment when I saw him. He was new and cute and caring—sweet, unlike some of the men I'd previously worked with. Immediately taken by him, it wasn't long before we began our now thirty-six year love affair. When we married, I asked Matt, my eldest half-brother, to be in the wedding party. Of course, my father and his family came too, bearing a gift. Perhaps I expected a more traditional gift, but that kind of thinking was never in unison with Dad's brood. A little skeptical, I excused myself to the bathroom and opened the package, which was long and shaped like a fountain pen container. I lifted out the beautiful liquid silver Navajo necklace, "Hmm, how nice." Then I remembered, one of my brothers had won it in a swim meet. *Beverly's hand, mind- fucking me again!*

I decided I no longer wanted Dad and his family in my life. I had my own now, and besides, they created too much turmoil. Fred and I moved to Oregon, to an area near Lake Oswego. I didn't disclose our whereabouts to 'Them'. No more energy would go in their direction. We stayed in a residential hotel until completion of our cottage. The phone was ringing as we were walking in, and I ran to pick it up.

"Hello."

"Why did you leave Arizona without telling me?"

I covered the phone and mouthed to Fred... "My father!" "Aah, ah," I said stuttering. "Fred was offered a job, and we had to leave, almost overnight." I wish I could have told him what I really thought. *I never want to see you or your family again.* Our conversation ended and I pulled the phone jack out of the wall.

The view from our front window of Mt. St. Helen's and Mt. Hood was breathtaking. Life settled into wonderful. Our phone number was unlisted, and we were thrilled to be pregnant. I loved living in paradise. Every morning my eyes saw something new from the window; nature abounded with trees and various animals. Then it happened…a package, sitting on the doorstep, addressed to me in my maiden name from Beverly. My heart sank. *How the hell did she find me?*

I waited for Fred to get home before opening it. "You do it," I said, handing him the box. "Here, why don't you open the envelope?" he said. Inside she'd stapled a check for $6.21, and wrote — for baby's layette. *She knew I was pregnant? And besides, what the hell can I buy for $6.21, a box of diapers?* Her letter went on to brag about my brother Rob's accomplishments, and how they'd given him a silver *Corvette. Good for him.* He graduated from the Air Force Academy. Fred opened the package; it was a re-gifted cookbook, signed by someone to her. *What unbelievable gall!*

Before Brian, our beautiful Irish- complexioned son was born, we sold our house in Oregon and moved. Again, we were cautious giving forwarding information but they seemed to know our every move. The week before I went into labor Mom came from Arizona to help with the baby. One afternoon, the doorbell rang and she answered it. When she returned, she carried a package from 'Them'. I hesitated opening it, but with her there, I felt safe, so I went ahead and tore off the paper. Inside was a scratched, dull, plastic box, the kind Bobbi pins come in. Something wrapped in blue *Kleenex* fell out, it was a tarnished demitasse spoon. Disgusted, I picked it up and threw it in the trash. *In retrospect, I wonder if possibly it was Dad's baby spoon.* It doesn't matter. They know too much about our life, and I don't care what they send. I'll chuck it or give it away.

Three months after Brian's birth, we moved to Louisville, Kentucky. Once more, we were fortunate to begin anew. Fred's prestigious job afforded us a dream home on a tree-lined street, full of Southern charm. I felt as though my problems, 'Them', were on the other side of the world. We were blessed again with a pregnancy, and while eagerly awaiting Mikie's birth, little thought was given to 'Them'. Spring came, and just before Derby, I noticed a dark blue car parked two doors up. A man wearing a suit and tie sitting inside, bowed his head pretending to not see me whenever I walked by. After three days, I asked the neighbors if they knew him–No was their unanimous response. Curiosity got the best of me, so I slipped out of the back door, and approached the car from behind. Leaning inside the open rear window, he acted startled when I said, "What are you doing here? I've called the police." Truthfully, I hadn't, but he hightailed it out of there. I wondered, *Beverly? No, maybe, nah, she wouldn't.*

Work transfers took us to Portsmouth, Virginia. Our serene new home was on an old plantation surrounded by moss covered oaks and swampland. I felt secure, having no reason to worry since there had been no contact from anyone in New Mexico. We lived peacefully for three years in Virginia, and then one more time Fred was transferred. This time to St. Charles, Missouri, a bedroom community outside St. Louis. My mother's family was from Missouri, and I felt a connection to my roots living there, and it was a great place to raise our sons. Two years passed without incident, until I saw another car much like the one in Kentucky parked on our cul-de-sac. Checking with the four families in our neighborhood, no one knew why he or it would be there. I grabbed my bird watching binoculars, marched into the front yard and stared at him. I pretended to be scribbling down his license plate. When he realized I was watching him, he revved his engine and zoomed away. To this day, I swear he was watching us, and I believe he was Beverly's covert informer.

In 1998, I was suffering with an unexplainable malady. My doctor asked if I could get my father's medical history. I hadn't contacted him in years, but I needed to get the information. I went to great effort to keep our home address secret—using Fred's office as the return address. His reply disclosed Beverly's death, and asked why I had abandoned him! Not a word about my inquiry.

The years of weird spying contributed to a little neurosis in me, and I couldn't help wondering if her death may have been why the surreptitious activity ended. I believe she was the driving force behind all the crap, but he was complicit, leaving her to sabotage our relationship. On some level, and in his own way, I believe he cared for me and wasn't able to stand up to or assure her there was nothing to fear.

I've arrived at a time in life where introspection seems the norm; I've learned to stand up for myself, not be afraid to ask questions and challenge when someone inappropriately confronts me. As for my parents, they were who they were; I wish they had been willing to tell me about their courtship, relationship and divorce. Nevertheless, I too must assume responsibility for not asking Mom and allowing Dad to dismiss my questions. As for inheritances, I was left some money, but not from Dad. It came from a three-generations-removed immigrant maternal uncle from Ireland. Apparently, he was a hard worker who lived meagerly in Chicago and saved his money. I found this out when I received a call from an attorney asking questions about my name, birth and other identifying facts. I told her there were numerous Catherine Muldoons in the St. Louis area. "No," she said without equivocation, "You're the one I'm looking for and in a few weeks you will receive a letter with more information." Sure enough, a large envelope came from a Chicago law office, and inside a check made out to me for six thousand dollars. I didn't feel right keeping it, so I called her and asked that she give it to those family members who knew him, but I had a request. Could she get a list of all the Gannon's and O'Hanlon's–my maternal ancestors, my family tree? It's rather ironic I'm receiving money from someone I didn't know existed, and likewise. What a crazy juxtaposition. *Gifts can come from unexpected sources, and gifts can be non-material, but overall, affirmation of self can be the most rewarding.*

My father's death notice in the Albuquerque paper read something like this...Max Feld of Albuquerque, New Mexico, husband of Beverly (deceased) and father of three sons, Matt, Tim and Rob, passed away October 9, 2003...

Holy crap, this is overwhelming...*I'm not sure if I want to know anymore.*

Pippy: "Lobster! Yuck!"

Epilogue

As the years pass, my memories fade. Luckily, I remember the wounds with soft, smooth edges rather than the harsh, sharp and cold, as first felt. My life has indeed changed in so many ways from the moment I found my father's love letters, until now. I lived these experiences, perhaps moving through life with lightening speed and not fully recognizing what was happening. I say this because I have tended to see things in only one light rather than from other points of view. You may find, as I have, that not everything is as it first appears. It was thrilling to realize I had a father, and add to that, three half-brothers. Time and travels allowed us to become familiar with one another through letters and the first face-to-face meeting. The blunt comments throughout the first visit, and the knowledge that my father found it necessary to have me investigated, all painted a questionable picture. I set that aside and allowed my new family another chance. As the months and years passed, and the gifts arrived, I doubted their intentions, keeping my hurt to myself rather than confronting him. That eventually led to my final choice: severing all contact with his family even if it meant not seeing my half-brothers, whom I had come to care for deeply. As the years rolled by, the daily rush of living left little time to think about 'Them'. I blamed him for the 'odd' things that happened. My anger centered on the knowledge that we were being watched–by whom, we never knew, but found it extremely unsettling. The gifts were unnerving and I attributed the blame for them to my father. Could I have been wrong? He was involved in investigations concerning our whereabouts, that I am certain. It is possible he honestly didn't understand why I wanted him out of my life, but someone else did, and she knew the answer, which I assume she took to her grave.

If not for writing my story, I may never have seen the possibility that I misjudged him. I opened my heart to another perspective of thinking about my father.

I'm enjoying writing and hope to write more…who knows, you may hear from me again…

Catherine Muldoon

Cathy

Mary Beal Berchem

I'm an adventurer and my childhood home on the banks of the Verde River fed my inquisitiveness. The abundant life provided specimens for dissection in my backyard lab: Pollywogs, Glow Worms, Hellgrammites and a plethora of bugs. Pretending to be a pioneer woman, cooking over an open campfire, and sleeping in the yard on old quilts made by my grandmother, watching the nightly shower of falling stars in the indigo night sky, and making a wish on each one fueled my curiosity.

I've flown on Air Force jets, sailed on America's Cup Yachts, interviewed Presidents and other well-known world leaders. However, sorrow and tragedy, including my oldest son's murder, Mother's Alzheimers and death, Dad's and my brother Lou's deaths, and my four breast cancer surgeries in 2009 and 2010, have not dampened my desire to learn and live.

A chance opportunity to work in radio opened doors which led to ownership and a career as a nationally syndicated radio talk show host, which took me to the four corners of the world.

My husband Mike and I live in Hollywood; we met Valentine's Day 2000 at a friend's wedding in Las Vegas. We're a blended family with six children, one grandchild and two rescue dogs.

Road to Red Hole

By

Mary Beal Berchem

*y mind and body were numb and still wafting around
somewhere – a place I never want to go again...*
Glancing around my parent's house, though not my childhood home, many things are similar: Dad's worn velour recliner,
Mom's pink silk brocade chair, and on every side table, innumer-
able photos of grandchildren. Morning smells of coffee perking
and bread toasting agitate my already upset stomach. The kids
are watching Saturday morning cartoons, and Dad sits at the
head of the table, wrestling the newspaper and waiting for Mom
to fix breakfast. As much as I try, I can't keep my eyes off the
shoebox-sized container. It's out of place, and shouldn't be here,
nor perched on one of Grandma Wombacher's dainty crocheted
doilies.

A photo of my deceased maternal grandparents on their fif-
tieth wedding anniversary hangs above the dining room buffet.
Their downcast gaze seems fixated on the rectangular funeral
box, which for some reason reminds me of pictures of stoic,
unsmiling plantation 'overseers' guarding the 'bale'. How the

package arrived, I don't remember. *Was it delivered, or did Gary bring it from Texas?*

My brother Lou, nine years older and a heavy smoker, grudgingly goes outside for a cigarette and deliberately slams the screen door. A smudge consumes every molecule of my 'child brain', the bang resurrects scary memories of awful thunder and lightning storms during our torrential summer monsoons. The giant cumulus clouds would build up in the afternoon over Black Mountain, foretelling fury long before the storm's arrival. An eerie feeling enveloped our house when the 'fire dragon' cast his sword and growled a deafening warning. I imagined his jagged bolt must have struck a transformer in the alley. Millions of tiny sparks filled the blackened sky. My terror caused goose bumps to erupt on my arms and I looked for a place to hide from the battle waging outside. Everywhere the lights were out, with the exception of the headlights of passing cars, which cast flickering, monster shadows across our living room ceiling.

Lou was ornery, and often used me as his foil. I remember once he assured Mom the movie we were going to see was non-objectionable, "I looked in the *Catholic Digest*," he lied. I was nine, and he was seventeen. We saw, "*The Curse of Frankenstein*," and that night, ghoulish images silhouetted from the leaf-bare trees wriggling outside my bedroom window terrified me and I called out for Mom. Pleading for her to come get in my bed, I could hear him giggling in his room. At the breakfast table, he'd kick my leg, grin, and call me a 'scaredy cat.' Those childhood days are long gone. Now, I love the powerful summer storms bringing their gift of precious liquid to our parched desert. However, this experience is terrifying too; in fact, it is pure havoc!

Brian David, my first-born son was twelve when he flew into the house one day after school and proclaimed, "From now on, I want to be called David." I didn't think it was a big deal; I'd done the same thing when I was a kid. I hated my name Mary Evelyn. At school, the kids called me "Mary Elephant." I would sneer and demand they call me, "Mary." It is no longer important if he was Brian or David, David or Brian, just that he was…

Five-fifteen sticks in my mind. I believe we had just sat down for Sunday dinner when the phone rang. Beverly, my former husband's wife said, "David's dead. He was murdered." Silence followed; I stood frozen. All I could think was, *Alison and Tre* (my younger children) *were in Tucson, and I have to call them. They must hear this from me, not someone else.* Alison answered on the first ring, and as I tried to explain, my words sounded like the adult-speak in *Charlie Brown* animations, that inarticulate, "waa,waa,waa" — senseless, gibberish.

"Mom, we know. Someone already called," she said, crying.

Like ocean tides, memories of life with David come and go, and as close as I can calculate, 'I' became 'we' two weeks after high school graduation. I was seventeen and determined to get out of town; freedom two hours away — Arizona State University. My first class, Psychology 101, was at 7:40 A.M. and in a few weeks, a wave of nausea came over me. It didn't feel like flu and repeated the next morning. Not wanting my professor to notice, I moved from the front row to an inconspicuous seat in back near the door. *Oh god, please don't let this be morning sickness.*

The disgusting smell of cigarettes crushed out in the glass ashtray sitting on the tan tiled floor next to my roommate's bed was sickening, and I begged our floor captain to move. "There aren't any open rooms on the freshman floor; however, there is one upstairs, but she's a sophomore...I'll ask anyway, and if it's okay with her, I'll bend the rules." *Lucky for me she's Mormon.* Fresh air flowing in from the open transom brought the sweet aroma of vetiver from the newly mowed grass below. Flopping on the bed, I finally rested–*sleep, glorious sleep.*

In 1965, 'safe sex' was the 'withdrawal' method. Now, I realize it was a miracle I didn't get pregnant sooner, because we'd been sexually active for three years. His metallic green 1960 *Ford Falcon* was our mobile 'love-nest'. The dark back roads on the outskirts of town provided seclusion for parking and sex. Birth control pills were available in the early sixties. However, I came from a small town, 400 people max, and would not have gone to our family doctor, or any doctor; embarrassment overruled my fear of pregnancy. Today, that's hard for me to imagine. My girlfriends and I snickered and joked about rubbers. *We were so gullible.* Our boyfriends had us believing the only time they needed a condom was screwing a whore. Truthfully, we'd heard about venereal diseases—gono, and syphilis—but only those slutty girls were diseased!

My last period had been two months ago, and the *possibility* was unthinkable. Terrified, and needing confirmation, I asked Sandra, Gary's pregnant sister, for her doctor's name and number. I made the appointment, and when I signed the patient's register as 'Mary Higby' I did so out of shame, knowing that I would be 'PG' as we called it, out of wedlock. The nurse said, "Call back in two days for the results." Walking out of the clinic, I wondered if it was true: a bunny rabbit would die. The test for pregnancy was injecting a woman's urine into a rabbit. There were no EPTs.

The only public phone in the dorm was in the hall across from the monitor's desk. I waited and waited for the chatty girls ahead of me to finish yakking. *Finally, my turn.* Grabbing the receiver, I turned my back to the others. My hopes disappeared like the dime I dropped into the slot when the voice on the other end said, "Congratulations, Mrs. Higby, your due date is the second week in February, do you want to make an appointment to see the doctor?" I never considered adoption or abortion. Marriage was the norm and that would be my only choice. I left the dorm looking for a private public phone. I needed to call Gary, who was living in Tucson with his parents and working during summer break. He agreed I should move to Tucson and we'd get married. My older sister Pat lived there and offered Dodi, my seven years younger niece's, bedroom. Memories of dresses Pat made for me when I was little zoomed light speed–today. Now after years of perfecting her art, she would sew my wedding dress. At the fabric store, we searched *Simplicity* pattern books, deciding on a simple A-line design. The material most suited to the style was heavy embossed white cotton. Instead of a veil, a shoulder-length *mantilla*, one Gary and I bought on a trip to Nogales, Mexico. He wore a white dinner jacket and a fuchsia rose boutonniere. Premarital classes were a prerequisite for a church wedding; however, Gary was non-Catholic and we were not permitted to have a wedding mass. The ceremony was in an enormous church, one of Tucson's largest. Elegant wrought iron chandeliers hanging from high rafters cast a diffused light throughout the quiet, vast space; sanctuary candles flickered on the altar and the walk began. During rehearsal, I counted thirty pews before arriving at the altar; however, on our wedding day, all were empty except the first two front rows.

"All rise," the priest said.

Someone was sobbing and I wanted to turn and see who, but kept my eyes on the priest. After the ceremony, I asked Pat, "Who was crying?"

"Dad," she said.

Pat's track home on the eastside would be the post nuptial–*locale celebratione*. I don't recall much of the to-do now, but one gift in particular stood out–an ironing board dressed like a woman: gray, dreadlock mop hair, hand-shaped potholder gloves, and apron. In addition, copper scouring pads–supposedly a traditional 1960 homemaker. *Ah, finale!* We hopped into the *Falcon*, beer and soda cans tied to the fender. Everyone waited to blast us with handfuls of rice. The late August heat left us sweltering inside the non-air-conditioned car plus facing the setting sun made the drive to Phoenix exhausting. We checked into the Kon-Tiki hotel, hurried to our room, cranked up the air-conditioning, tore off our clothes, made love, and ordered club sandwiches from room service.

The next day real life began. Our honeymoon was spent moving into a one-bedroom apartment near campus. Fall semester started Monday.

The Village Market, a short twenty minute walk away became a weekly ritual on my day off from class. I looked forward to seeing the friendly people whom I'd become familiar. Especially, the butcher Carl, who had taken a liking to me, and would often tease me about my frugal purchases–*Campbell's* soup, prunes, tomato sauce, spaghetti noodles, milk, bread and butter. Many times, he'd slip a package into the cart thinking I hadn't noticed. Truthfully, he never slipped anything by me. It was our little game. Honestly, I couldn't wait to get home and unwrap the surprise. Usually there were better cuts of meat disguised as eighty-nine cents a pound ground beef. His affection for me meant we would eat round steak, pork chops or chicken breasts. By the time I started wearing maternity clothes which was about six months, I recall him saying, "When the baby comes, bring him or her in, and I'll give you the best steaks in the house."

Labor started early in the morning. Unaware, I slept through the first stages. Suddenly, I felt a gripping stab in my abdomen and sat up in bed. Gary, startled awake now grabbed his watch and started timing the contractions — twenty minutes apart. "If this is what it's like to have a baby, I never want another child," I shrieked. "We'd better go to the hospital," he said. Much to our disappointment, a stern nurse sent us home only to endure four more hours of torture before my contractions were five minutes apart. "Jesus, I can't stand this anymore. Take me to the hospital, now!" The labor room was full of moaning and screaming women lying on narrow carts in cubicles surrounded by sliding canvas drapes and waiting in agony until dilated and given the *go* for the delivery room. A nurse handed me a silver flashlight-looking tube with a triangular black padded breathing mask on one end. "Here," she said, "Push this button and take deep breaths when the pain starts." I sucked and sucked until my mind became fuzzy and the overhead lights blurred and distorted. All I remember was hearing the doctor say, "Let's get her into delivery." He said something else, but his voice sounded far away and in slow motion. "Mary, I'm going to use something to help ease the baby out." Horrific torturous cutting...*the episiotomy*. Searing hot poker rammed inside...*the forceps*. Nightmarish hallucinations of brilliant fluorescent colors flooded my head...*Baby crying, baby crying*. The pain subsided. "Mary"...*unclear*, "Mary, you have a baby boy. He weighs seven pounds five ounces and is twenty one and a half inches long." A nurse laid him on my stomach wrapped in a white, pink and blue blanket. "Here's your bundle of love," she said. I gasped when I saw the huge red horseshoe-shaped mark on his right forehead and under his eye, the brand left from the forceps. I cried, fearing it permanent, but the doctor reassured me it would fade in a week or two, and it did.

Gary left the waiting room eager to call our parents with the happy news. When he returned, he said, "All your Mother said, in her inimitable way was...'how nice, and are they doing well?'"

Dismayed by her remark, I asked, "Did she say they were coming?"

"Your Dad and Dot Pot (Mom's best friend) are, but your Mom didn't say anything."   "What, she's still pissed?"

"No, Dot thinks she's embarrassed because the baby was born six months after our wedding."

"Which one is the Higby baby?" Dad's voice resonated. I peeked around the door and saw the nurse holding Brian up. Dad, now Papo tapped on the window, and baby Brian opened his eyes. Dad, Mom and Dot stood before the nursery window 'oohing and ahhing' and making silly faces. Mom, now Mamo, having been stoic and indifferent, fell in love.

I hate that damn box. It reminds me of the black monolith in "2001: A Space Odyssey," and it's just as ominous. The memorial service lasted a half an hour, and everyone filed out of St. Cecilia's Catholic Church. Most blessed themselves with holy water from the marble fount and waited solemnly outside. When I stepped through the door the first people I noticed were Fermin and Cruz Estrada, David's Padrino and Madrina (godparents), standing off to the side. They held each other, heads hanging, shaking and wiping their eyes. Other people with woeful faces stared at me. I disliked being the center of attention, but smiled perfunctorily and expressed my thanks for coming. Now, Gary and I would take our son to the place where all this would end.

David was killed when I was thirty-nine. He was living in Hurst, Texas, and attending college in nearby Denton. The Arlington police report stated they were called to investigate a disturbance; however, when they arrived and found nothing out of the ordinary, they left. Then calls started coming in reporting horrific yelling and screaming from the apartment of the earlier call-out. Once again, they returned. Now, aware something indeed had taken place, they noticed suspicious deep grooves in the grass leading from one of the apartments and toward the nearby ravine. Following the drag-marks, they discovered my son's lifeless body. The investigators said they returned to the apartment where they found a disheveled and disoriented man sitting among pieces of broken furniture and bloody clothes. The police report stated David's death was due to blunt force trauma to the left side of his head, and the murder weapon was most likely a baseball bat found at the scene. They also noted he'd been choked with a belt.

I chose not to go to the trial. The thought of seeing the face of the man who murdered him was unbearable and I didn't want it to be indelibly etched in my mind. Justice would come from the people of Texas, hearing the evidence and deciding the perpetrator's fate. My recollection of the trial's outcome was a conviction of murder and sentence of twenty-five years to life in prison. Years later, I learned he served seventeen and was released on parole. Authorities have told me he re-offended and spent a couple of years in a Kansas correctional facility, and is again out on parole.

Our families dearly loved David. We had many happy times celebrating birthdays, and holidays when he was little. I remember with special fondness the time we gave him his first fishing pole. The determination in his eyes tickled me. With his jaw set, pole and hook in one hand, and chicken liver bait in the other, he cast the line out to the deepest bend on the far side of the river. He never sat still, but now, sat patiently holding the rod ever so gently, and staring at the bobber until, 'bloop,' down it went. He jumped up and yanked the line to set the hook and began turning the knobs on the reel, yelling, "He took it, I got him!" It was a shiny, gray-whiskered channel cat. We cheered, as he reeled in the struggling fish. He clasped its slippery body and removed the hook without being stung, then put it in the creel. He picked up his pole, put the creel strap over his head and shoulder, and said, "Let's go, I wanna eat it." Gary helped skin, gut and filet the fish, then David handed me two small pieces, which I dredged in egg and cornmeal, and fried in Mom's cast iron skillet. The nugget was too hot for him to bite; which afforded me time to grab my *Kodak Instamatic* and take one of my favorite pictures of him: that quirky little grin, with those upturned and pursed lips curling into a sweet dimple on his left cheek. His sparkling eyes told all—satisfaction—job well done.

When David was nine, Gary and I divorced. Gary had been an Air Force pilot, and his assignments took him all over the world, which resulted in long periods away from home. He later became an airline pilot–we eventually grew apart. Twelve years later our hearts breaking, we were taking our son's ashes to Red Hole where we agreed he should rest. My cousin Steve, Gary's best friend, led the way in his pick-up truck along the rickety dirt road to Sycamore Canyon. Driving behind, billowing clouds of dust engulfed our car. *I haven't been to this place in years.* As Steve turns off the road onto an obscure path, our car bottoms out on a berm left by the monthly swipe by the county road grader. Gary gunned the engine and the car shot over the hump, but not before the box started tilting. I braced it firmly between my feet until we arrived at the familiar steep-walled box canyon. I had forgotten how unnerving it was, standing close to the edge and peering over. Feeling vertigo, I stepped back. Gary lifted the *scourge* out of the car, and set it on the ground. When he pried off the top, I gasped because I'd never had I seen cremated remains: bone fragments and tooth remnants sitting atop chunky gray powder. Together we held the box and poured out his ashes. A breeze grabbed them, forming an S-shaped ripple, which swirled downward and settled into Red Hole. I don't remember much from that point on–not going to the airport or arriving back in Kansas.

Two weeks passed, and I returned to work at the radio station. I was surprised that only a few of my peers asked what happened, or how I was doing. It was as though the door slammed and what was before was no more. I've come to realize that people don't know what to say; it's an unusual and uncomfortable situation. I too have hesitated asking for fear I might be intruding on someone's pain. However, I needed to talk until I'd exhausted the need. Alone and hiding my grief, I was desperate to find someone who would understand what I was going through. A friend, whose child died of Leukemia, told me about a group called *Compassionate Friends.* While attending the first meeting, I felt as though I belonged. Other parents described their losses;

one woman lost her entire family in a house fire, and others lost children in car accidents or to cancer or other diseases. But, when parents whose child committed suicide told their stories, I was bewildered and wondered how they survived. As time passed, I began to understand and realized that, like them, I must find meaning in my life. They suggested I do something positive–help those in need, volunteer, and create a new way to honor his life. I didn't know what that might be and kept thinking, *parents are supposed to die before their children, regardless of whether they're three, twenty-three, or sixty-three.* Guilt plowed its way through me. What could I have done to prevent his death was a persistent question that came knocking on those sleepless nights, and has never abated. Twenty-two years later, I am visited by the 'guilt intruder' now less frequently, but it still gnaws away at my conscience. Shortly after his death I dreamed about him; it seemed very real and I've analyzed and dissected it to no avail.

A noise woke me. It was early morning and light was eking through the blinds. I sat up and was aghast...Sally, David's long-dead silver and black haired German shepherd, stood in the doorway staring at me. I patted the bed, she jumped up, and I began petting her soft warm body. I told her how happy I was to see her. Her expressive caramel brown eyes explained telepathically that she and David were together and well, and didn't want me to worry anymore. After that experience, I felt different; it was as though he had released me.

His death thrust upon me suddenly, was torture. However, as tragic as it was, I didn't see him suffer, or kept alive artificially with no quality of life; I was spared the decision of pulling the plug on my child. I grieved, trying to make sense of it, but there was none. I vowed not to become immersed in anger or focus on retribution. My body ached, and all I felt was deep sorrow. I keep my memories of him in an imaginary purple velvet and gold drawstring bag, cradled inside a special place in my heart.

I was a very young mother, and sometimes we acted more like big sister and little brother. We played tag, hide and go seek, and built forts with blankets: crawling inside, sitting cross-legged and pretending the ghoulish faces we'd make from holding flashlights under our chins were monsters coming to get us. His favorite song was, "*Yummy, yummy, yummy I've got love in my tummy.*"[2] He'd say, "Pway it again, Mommy."

As a teenager, he preferred *Billy Idol* and *Blue Oyster Cult,* and once in awhile I see a car that looks exactly like his 1969 Z28 dark blue *Camaro* with gold racing stripes. I can't help looking to see who is driving.

The eleven days between his birthday, February 10, and his death day February 21, my mood is reserved, introspective, and I think about him more than usual. While secreted in the shower or awake in the middle of the night, tears run down my cheeks, and just like the song by *Jackie Wilson,* "*Lonely Teardrops,*" my pillow never dries. Cherished memories of him fishing, and pretending he was *Evel Kneivel* riding his orange raised-handlebar bike, jumping over ramps of stacked cardboard boxes—his toothless first grade photo evidence of his wild bike riding. Another time, red ants escaped from the gigantic *Plexiglas* ant farm he kept near his bedroom window. Apparently, they devised a way out through the half-open window. His most memorable antic happened when Carmen, our housekeeper, stomped out of his bedroom, looking disgusted, and shoving a box at me, saying in perturbed Spanish, "No, bien!" After trying to calm her down, she said she'd been dust mopping under his bed when the box flew out. Understandably insulted by his stash of multi-colored condoms, some wrapped, and others opened like deflated balloons. I fumed, waiting for him to get home from school. The minute I heard him open the door, I was right there demanding, "What the hell is a seventh grader doing with rubbers, and where did you get these damn things?" "Well, I get them from the vending machines in the men's bathrooms when we go out to eat."

Twenty-one years of life is brief, compared to my sixty plus. I often think of how fleeting those times were, and wish precious moments could be reduced to a pill and taken again as re-experience. David's life was much more than I can tell. He was blessed with physical beauty, but demons beyond my knowing or

---

2 The Ohio Express, 1968, Yummy, yummy, yummy, I've got love in my tummy.

understanding made his life difficult. He didn't conform, wasn't a good student, and searched for more than could be given or found. His light started to dim when he was twelve and, while we were visiting relatives in Alaska, marijuana shared by the older teens hooked him. I believe he had a genetic pre-disposition to alcohol and drugs that led him on a downward spiral. His high school years were not stereotypical. His friends weren't class-mates, they were older, and kids who'd dropped out. We tried every means to discourage his relationships with those people. He went into counseling; we tried tough love, and drug treat-ment at one of the most renowned rehab facilities in the coun-try. Helplessness turned to futility. As with many addicts, David would rebound, then relapse, and each time we hoped it would be the one that worked. He decided Texas and college would be his opportunity to start anew. With great expectation, we hoped and prayed he was right. The last time I saw him, we looked into each other's eyes and said, "I love you, and will miss you," neither of us knowing it would be goodbye forever. I'd sensed foreboding before, and I think most parents experience this feel-ing whenever their child jumps into a car and heads away from home.

After working eight years in Wichita, my company trans-ferred me to Jacksonville, Florida. When some of my friends learned I was leaving, they asked if they could give me a going away party. I was honored by their gesture, but wanted it to be more than a party for me; however, I was concerned they'd turn it into a surprise if I said no. I suggested we make it a party with a purpose. Out of that idea, The Brian David Higby Fund was born. It was not only a heartfelt farewell, but it gave me a life-long tie to the community who'd done so much for me.

In the beginning, the fund's goal was to help disadvantaged middle school children attend summer camp or participate in other enrichment activities. It has evolved to where it contin-ues to provide funds for this, but also helps children of abuse. Hundreds of kids have benefitted from David's fund. It has been seventeen years, and now, the tears I cry are of joy, seeing my son's face in the eyes of each child, and knowing that if not for his death, I might never have had this privilege.

David would be forty-five had he lived, and I miss not knowing the man he would become, and wonder what our lives would be had he not died. Perhaps, he'd be a husband or father. Would his children look like him? Would we build forts out of blankets and play the same games? Would they call me Grandma, Gramma, or possibly Mamo?

I suppose I've reconciled his death, but on occasion, there are uncertainties about choices I made. *Could I have done something more?* I emphatically disagree when people talk about 'closure.' It's cliché and untrue. I don't like hearing, "He's in a better place," or "It's God's will." I'd rather have someone simply say, "I'm sorry for your loss," and leave it at that.

All that is certain is my life moves on day to day, year to year, and my child is dead. I'm not cynical, but truthfully, until my dying breath, I won't know anymore about dying and the hereafter than I do today.

David's death is my story, and I'm one of countless mothers who've buried murdered children. Regardless of how statistically similar our stories might sound, the details of each are unique. I don't feel their pain; I'm reminded of mine.

Sally
"David and I are together."

David
"Today's limit!"

"You should write a book." Comments made over the years from those listening to my stories. However, when they're your stories, they're just that. Nothing extraordinary, just who I am and what I've done. Furthermore, I was raised with the belief that talking about me–or worse, bragging–was akin to sin. It is interesting being the one asking those questions now, and encouraging others to tell their stories and getting the same response.

Truth: nothing is uttered that is not thought, be it verbalized or written. How else would our civilization be where it is today if not for someone telling a story, their story?

Using the age-old-excuse—there are more important and interesting people—that, coupled with doubt, fear, and lacking confidence—how could I write, let alone write a book. I wouldn't know where to begin. I started jotting down things I'd done as a kid. However, the morning I saw Mom's face in the magnifying mirror, I knew it was time to get off my fanny.

After calling friends about the apparition, I had, as Oprah calls it, the light bulb moment. I was recovering from breast cancer, and thoughts were running rampant—what should I do with all this buzzing in my head? Perhaps, now was the time to learn. I hired a writing coach and started–simply started. Which by the way, most writers agree is the hardest part. I remember a friend of my husband, writer James Ellroy, saying, "All that separates writers from non-writers are that the ones who write. So just do it." I wanted to write my memories well. I'm pleased when it flows from my brain, through my hands and to the page without strain or great deliberation. I am filled with delight, laugh aloud, sit back in my inexpensive brown fake leather office chair, cross my arms, and howl. *How could I have composed this piece, this aria?*

If no one were to read what I've written, the personal satisfaction derived from the entire process made me a different person. Confidence no longer means proving something to someone. I've never had difficulty telling, recalling my brother in law's endearing, "Mary, you have diarrhea of the mouth" comment. I needed to learn the method of memoir writing—not so easy. I've not committed to anything with the same intensity and drive. The time it takes, coupled with many moments of frustration could have easily resulted in giving up. Nevertheless, I did not, and the more I write, the more I want to write. Moreover, if not for those friends who journeyed with me, I am not sure I would be writing today. They exemplify the meaning of friendship—love, trust, honesty, forgiveness and faith. To them I am forever grateful.

Mary Beal Berchem

Mary

Frankie Boyer

The canvas is me; I create my life, as would a painter revealing brush strokes of compassion, devotion, pain and insight into my work. Color, texture, mood and awareness fill me with inspiration. My life's aspiration is to be a beacon for physical, mental and spiritual health. I'm forever searching for truth and enlightenment to share with my radio listeners.

Learning about my twin sister who died at birth, estrangement from friends and family, putting my well-being in jeopardy by giving and helping others out of their problems, loosing most of my inheritance, falling in love with someone who would never be mine, and trying my entire life to be the beauty I was told I wasn't has been more than challenging. I've never been married. I love dogs, and Tutu my black Chow was the love of my life. I live in Boston.

Frankelinky

By

Frankie Boyer

Sparkle always arrived before she entered

and

all who knew her noticed some dimming.

Signs were dismissed

just coincidence

she wasn't young anymore.

Years of sucking on non-filtered *Herbert Tarringtons*

gifted *COPD* with its insidious cough, tiredness and

labored breathing.

Life was hard, but no harder than anyone else

whose losses were numerable under the age of 46.

Deaths of parents, children, and Dad

and now, beloved companion

'Me Too.'

Black bundle of Poodle-love never far away

or out of her sight

filling Ma's heart and soul with just enough spunk

a drop of adrenaline

refreshing like water on a drooping Pothos.

The racing old Caddie dealt the final blow

the already disastrous open gate — the hangman.

"I am never going to bury anyone, ever again," Mother said.

Seven days of sadness

after Me Too's murder was unbearable.

Unexpectedly hospital one, then hospital two became Betty's

sleeping quarters —

barracks where time tolled — almost over.

Six weeks!

Wondering why she didn't respond?

Questions burning

I prodded the Doctors.

Indifferent

chatting among themselves and perplexed by her purplish-black

fingertips and toes.

Tubes, buzzers, machines with wavy red and yellow lines and

the clear round vessel

playing its accordion tune—up—down—swoosh—swoosh–

alerting her every breath.

"We'll have to amputate!" They agreed, shaking their heads.

How, dear god, how will I tell her?

"Over my dead body," she'd shriek.

Long manicured nails and pearly white polish as

far back as I remember.

The half-open drawer displays necessities:

emery board, tweezers, and *Cutex*: Opalescent White.

Feigning pleasant,

"Ma, is there anything I can do for you?"

"Pluck these hairs."

"Oh, Ma no one can see them

they're white, almost invisible."

"Yes, I know, but I can feel them."

Sun worshipper in winter

snow covering the ground below our deck

sitting, tanning, bronzing… "I need a little color," she'd say.

Hands now transparent, skinny, bulging veins and dotted with

continent shaped blotchy brown flecks.

Resting my hand on hers

close in size, but not exactly identical

those same irregular spots.

Memories pour tears, thoughts, feelings

wiping wet from cheek onto tissue and wondering,

"Ma, do you love me, are you proud of me?"

Minds transfuse daughter to mother.

She tapped the bed

I obliged and bent over

so close, I felt little warmth

and

smelled the uncommon mix of

hand lotion, sulfur, ammonia, rotten eggs, water dumped from

vases of wilted flowers

her scent.

Hands caressing my face

not rough, not smooth nor soft

but

I know velvet, satin and silk.

"Frankelinky"

You have brought me joy and love

precious baby girl — last born.

I am a proud Mother.

Now it's her curtain call

Preparations for the finale begin.

A nurse never before seen

carefully swabbed Mother's mouth

adjusted sheets and blanket

and

one by one, sounds lessened.

Quiet.

She whispered in Ma's ear, "Betty, your baby is here to take you

home."

Humming an unfamiliar tune

she danced about the room,

touching Ma and smoothing her hair and tidying up.

Might she be an angel

sent to guide Ma on her journey?

All was done

and

I crawled in bed next to her,

kissing

hugging

and reassuring

Dad, Louis, Ritchie, Baby Boyer (my unnamed twin), Rosie,

Abe, Barney, Molly

and

'Me Too' awaited.

Pain turned to peace

she was radiant.

*"Some mothers are kissing mothers and some are scolding mothers,
but it is love just the same, and most mothers kiss and scold together."*
Pearl S. Buck

Frankie at her brother's bar mitzvah
"Already a talker!"

Betty and Me Too.

Epilogue

I've broadcast my radio program from the Natural Food Expo held in the Anaheim Convention Center across the street from Disneyland for many years. In addition, lucky for me, Mary, my friend lives a few minutes away in the adjacent city of Fullerton. I steal a little time the final day to see her before going back to Boston. We comment on how it seems only weeks since last seeing each other, when in reality it has been over a year. This year things changed, much as life changes. Mary now lives in Los Angeles and the drive is no longer minutes — hours.

We met years ago at a Talk Radio convention and have been friends since, sharing, supporting each other and discussing ideas of what we could do to assist women. So, when Mary called and told me about a vision she'd had of seeing her dead mother's face in the magnifying mirror and questioned whether I'd experienced anything similar plus her proposal about going to Santa Fe and meeting with other friends who'd agreed to tell their stories, I said, "Just let me know when." I began thinking about unexplored feelings, and questioning experiences, mostly sad, unanswered and filled with self-doubt about my relationship with my mother. It's been three years of opening closets, and walking through fires of grief, sorrow, pain, and hurt. Now, with veiled layers peeled away and viewing my life with adult perception, I embraced "Little Frankie", and her child's mind full of misunderstandings.

Mother, Betty Boyer, was a formidable woman and I too am independent and self-sufficient. After writing my story, I realized her legacy was giving me the tools necessary to push forward through hard times. She was not a lovey, touchy, kissy, full of compliments mother, rather, one who gave her personal wisdom instead of a baby book full of cute little incidentals.

If I could choose her to have been different, I can truly say without hesitation, "I don't think so."

The overwhelming need of hearing her validation, acknowledgement and affection came when I crawled into her hospital bed and laid my head on her shoulder. With her thin, frail hands, she cradled my face and bestowed her final gift—feeding my heart. Shortly thereafter, she died.

If not for allowing myself to explore all the feelings and heal the wounds through the looking glass of this journey, I may not have learned how to get from "Frankie—Frankelinky." I had used unknowing for nourishment, and the pounds piled on physically and emotionally. The holes I dug were getting deeper and deeper; however, as I wrote, understanding led to clarity. When the ah-ha moment arrived, I felt lighter, started losing weight and learned how to eat good, nutritious food. I began writing with ease, my paintings brightened and people complimented how I had captured sensitivity and beauty in my subjects. Then to my surprise, I noticed my voice sounded confident.

I believe we have an inherent need to connect, and I found those people who embraced and accepted me, allowing me to be me.

Frankie Boyer

Frankie

Pamela Bjork

Wanderlust and lure of the unfamiliar had me at an early age. I've walked five continents in red shoes like Dorothy's, reminding me *I'm not in Kansas anymore*. Spiritual quests took me to Tibet to witness a sky burial/funeral at 15,000 ft. I have experienced initiation with Santeria *babalawos* in Havana, visited tribal cultures in Ethiopia and walked alongside the grief-stricken during *The Procession of the Mysteries in Sicily*. Pilgrimage to Black Madonna sites in France and Spain helped heal me. Bali beckoned with her resplendent textiles and healers who exorcised demonic spirits. Along the way, I attended UC Berkeley in the late 60's and spent 22 years as a restaurateur in Colorado and Kansas. My immediate family's deaths were suicide, murder and cancer. My two sons, now adults, share my passion for food and travel. Recently, I completed a Ph.D. in Cultural Mythology and live in Santa Barbara, California.

My Toto *is Auchen*, a blue-eyed Border collie, always by my side.

She Walked in Beauty

By

Pamela Bjork

Listen to schizophrenic stories – there's justice in that.
– C. J. Jung

"No way, Mom," Justin said when I asked him to remove the black cat from our doorstep. I leaned over to pick up the morning paper and there it was, a large black cat curled on its side, its tail resting on the sisal welcome mat. I gingerly nudged it with my foot. It was stiff. Justin ran inside, slamming the glass door. I wasn't far behind.

"Garrett," I called to my younger son even though I knew the chance of him helping was zilch. Justin had already tipped him off and nothing short of a tornado would pull Garrett away from his *Honey Nut Cheerios*.

"You're guys! You're supposed to do these kinds of things."

"No way, Mom," I heard in unison.

Unable to dispose of the corpse, I left the house wishing the unfortunate creature would miraculously disappear by the time we returned home. I dropped Garrett off at school, hoped Justin would attend his high-school classes, and then drove to work. It was a busy day at the restaurant; I forgot about the cat until later that night when I opened the front door, my heart a flutter, and saw it lying in the same position. Again, I couldn't bring myself to move it, let alone, bury it.

While serving Justin macaroni and cheese that evening, he said, "I bet that cat means something creepy is going to happen."

A feeling of dread swept through me. I wondered if its dying on my doorstep was an omen that something bad might happen. *Maybe someone has it out for me? Was it a sign of the devil or black magic?* I thought about my dead brother, who twenty-three years before, was found face down on a Texas beach with a bullet in his head. He was twenty-two; I was twenty-six when he died. The Navy said he committed suicide. Then there was Donna, my paranoid schizophrenic sister, two years younger than I.

I hid my anxiety from the boys, going to work as usual, and they to school. For two days, we left and entered the house through the garage door, hoping the black cat would vanish from our porch as mysteriously as it had appeared. Nevertheless, its ominous presence remained. I awakened each morning with a gnawing premonition that this was a sign, of what I had no idea, but I knew it wasn't good.

One wintry Sunday afternoon two months earlier, Donna knocked at my front door, catatonic, a disconnected stare replacing her once vibrant blue eyes, her blond hair dirty and disheveled.

"Can I stay with you?" she asked, her eyes not meeting mine.

"Okay."

I took her by the hand, and led her to the guest bedroom. She was like a frightened child, our parents and brother were deceased and there was no one else for her to turn to. Donna had recently fired her psychologist of twenty years, saying he couldn't help her, that he was a crook and had used her to finance his daughter's college education, which may or may not have been true. However, I was in no position to care for her. I was a single mom raising two ornery boys, over-extended and exhausted from trying to keep my own life together, dealing with my restaurant, and trying to save my parents' dealership from takeover by *Chrysler Corporation*. At times, I felt on the verge of breakdown. Yet, I couldn't collapse. *Who would care for my sons, my restaurant, my customers, and my parents' hard-earned business?*

I both hated and loved my sister, and wondered why she couldn't pull herself together and will away her moods. If I could do it, so could she. "Have a stiff upper lip," Frankie, our mother, used to say. Go to work even if you're sick—that's what our family did—until now. I judged her weak and feigned compassion. I felt responsible for her and resented her intrusion.

Long gone were those childhood days when Donna and I giggled in our upstairs bedroom. On Saturdays after dusting and vacuuming, Donna and I would ride the ten-cent bus to downtown Wichita, stop at *Woolworth's* soda fountain for cherry cokes and window-shop until it was time to head home. I taught Donna to smoke *Winston's* from the red, half-full pack I stole from Frankie's purse. Our *Pepto-Bismol* pink bathroom was the hiding place for our nefarious activity. I cracked the window over the sink a couple of inches and we blew out the smoke. I loved her then—she wasn't supposed to go mad or get locked up in psychiatric hospitals. *Weren't we meant to be friends forever?*

Donna didn't eat with us that Sunday evening or the next day, either. She rarely came downstairs; instead, she lay motionless on the guest room bed, blanketed in our grandmother's wedding-ring quilt. Trying to make normal this aberrant situation, the boys went to school and I to work. *How long could we keep this up?* I had no idea how to handle her 'Jekyll and Hyde' moods or her screaming down the stairs "I hate you" one moment, then the next day cuddling beside me on the couch to watch *The X-Files*. I never really accepted my sister's mental illness and naïvely hoped she would change and be healed of her psychosis. After three days with us, I finally understood she couldn't care for herself she needed professional help.

Fortunately, her psychiatrist lived across the street, though we only knew each other in passing. Realizing I had nowhere else to turn, I rang his doorbell. "Donna needs help," I pleaded. "I don't know what to do, she's not taking her meds and now she's locked up in her room and won't talk."

"Alright," he said, grabbing his bag, and racing to my house. "Where is she?"

I led him upstairs and pointed... "In there."

"Please leave us alone; patient confidentiality," he said.

Reluctantly, I went downstairs. After half an hour, he came down and handed me a piece of paper, "This order will admit her to the lock-down ward at Charter." Suddenly, the horrors of seeing her in a straight jacket, locked up in the window-less psych-ward two years after our brother died brought up regressed memories. I knew in my heart this was the right decision, so I packed her *Tumi* bag and Justin helped her downstairs and into the car. She sat in the front seat looking defeated; glazed eyes and head hung. I absorbed her despair consumed by the unbearable silence as we drove to the hospital. Once inside, Donna was unable to hold a pen, so I filled out the admission forms and held her shaking hand while she scribbled her name. I told her I loved her, and watched as the attendants escort her away disappearing behind locked doors. I stepped outside; the sun hit my face and warmed my freezing body, cold from the 'meat-locker' temperature inside. *Maybe this time she'll recover?*

She stayed a month, and received experimental medication aimed at keeping her thought and mood disorders at bay: drugs to ward off voices, drugs to counteract those drugs. *Drugs, drugs, and more drugs.* Lithium, the standard treatment for her disorder, became toxic: she couldn't take it anymore. I equated her situation to a *Molotov* cocktail of lethal prescriptions.

My once gentle sister had become a stranger over the past twenty years. Schizophrenia, like flesh-eating bacteria, was devouring her mind. After our father died, I recall her yelling at me, "I hate you! You have a successful business and two sons. I have nothing." My heart broke for both of us. Crossing my arms over my chest–armor protecting the scorching arrows she'd shot my way.

One day, Garrett and I brought her *Jelly Bellies*, she met us in the visitor's room and when I handed them to her, she threw the bag across the room. Looking like a flood ripping through the room, the rainbow colored candies scattered under furniture, everywhere! We never knew what to expect, she was like a zombie.

Would this cruel and merciless disease pass to my sons? Would I be next? The only thing I'd been told was that schizophrenia was a bio-chemical imbalance in the brain, and at the time the popular theory. Her doctors weren't allowed to give me any personal information, even though I was her *only* next of kin. I was reluctant to find out more about her illness. I thought if I left it alone, it might go away, just as I hoped the dead black cat would go away. I felt powerless and afraid, thinking I was to blame for her condition. I had children and a successful business that I loved and she never hesitated to rub that in.

Donna adored my sons, and over the years, she took them camping and hiking; her illness controlled by her meds allowed her to do these things. Together, Aunt Donna and my boys pitched tents in the woods, built bonfires, roasted hot dogs, and burned marshmallows to make gooey s'mores.

She was always kind to them; they told me they never experienced her rage. Garrett said, "Mom, I think she was mad about being in the hospital the time she threw the jellybeans." *Maybe so*, I thought, grateful he had seen it that way, since I'd taken it personally and was angry. Justin visited her once a week, and only when I made him—Sundays. He was off in his own teen-age world, lusting after his girlfriend, and chased by police while driving 100 miles an hour on the turnpike; which violated probation from stealing some stereo equipment.

Thirty days after admittance to the hospital, Donna was released–supposedly healed. She carried bottles of new drugs, a combination of stuff almost rendering her lifeless. Alongside her diminishing awareness, she almost reached the limit on her in-patient insurance. We drove to her white-shingled house, in silence. I unlocked the front door and helped her inside, then unpacked her favorite groceries. My greatest wish was that she would be okay. However, deep down I knew she couldn't manage alone. Arrangements were made for a nurse to check on her every couple of days. In the meantime, I called the Menninger Clinic in Topeka, renowned for its exceptional residential care.

I remember leaving her house and glancing back; she was curled in a fetal position on the couch. I felt sick. *How can life be so cruel? How can I leave her? I have to get back to my sons and my life.* Thank god, a few weeks later the Menninger said they could take her, but she refused to go.

Although Dad had grown her stock portfolio to over a million dollars, she was paranoid about spending it. His proclamation came on a Sunday afternoon after our traditional pot-roast dinner. "I made your sister a million dollars," boasting, while lying in his king-sized bed, wearing always-pressed pajamas, his crooked grin evidence of a brain tumor removed thirty years ago. *What about me, I'm your daughter too, and your grandsons?* I held my tongue. I realized it was an off-handed compliment in a way, so I justified. He believed I could care for myself. He trained me well; I started work in his business when I was twelve, filing service repair orders for ten cents an hour Sunday afternoons at the dealership.

On Wednesday, two days after the dead black cat showed up, I called animal control. They instructed me to carry it out to the street and it would be picked up with the trash on Friday. None of us could manage that, so while at the dealership that afternoon, I asked John, who'd been our porter for twenty-five years, "Can you, please come by my house and help move a cat off our porch?"

"Oh, Miz Pam, that's spooky! But, I'll do it for you, 'cuz I loved your Mama and she'd want me to help you and your boys." He arrived first thing the next morning. I held my sides laughing as I watched him jump up and down, scared. Then as he shoveled the carcass into a garbage bag and dragged it to the curb, he turned and said, "Whoa, Miz Pam, this cain't be good!" A creepy premonition of death crept over me and I tried to push it out of my mind. We stood on my front porch shaking our heads. The deed was done. He asked, "How's Miz Donna? I do miss her since your mama and papa died. She don't come to work no more."

"Well, John, she's taking wood-working classes and volunteers at the Art Museum." In the spirit of my mother, I dug in my wallet's secret pocket, and pulled out a crisp fifty-dollar bill and put it in his still-shaking hand. I gave him a big hug and said, "Oh, John, I can't thank you enough."

Something continued to haunt me. My sister called yesterday afternoon, she sounded optimistic, and with clarity I hadn't heard in the past. "I'm getting well, I'm okay now."

"That's great, Donna," I said, not knowing what else to say, and wanting desperately to believe her. However, her call felt peculiar. She'd had spells of 'normal' in the past. She was a good student and usually made A's. She likes working with her hands—making things out of clay, firing them in her kiln, constructing "nature-scapes" of ceramic bears frolicking in the woods complete with miniature pine trees–every little detail. She worked with power tools building benches, sanding them smooth so there wouldn't be rough spots and staining them warm earthy colors. Other times, she'd go cross-country skiing in Colorado. She'd pick Justin and Garrett up and off they'd go to the *Nu-Way* sandwich shop for their crumbly burgers, curly fries and root beer floats, afterwards they'd visit the *Children's Art Museum*.

Making matters worse, I'd just written a sizable check to the IRS leaving me with a hundred dollars until payday. Justin was awaiting sentencing for his probation violation, which distracted me with worry—*would he be sent to prison or 'juvie'?* The dealership was in the red, and my restaurant staff was stealing food and booze. When I got home, I felt like a rag-doll, devoid of energy, and needing a reprieve from all this chaos. *If only I had some ruby slippers… I'd click my heels and disappear to some magical place.*

The phone rang and it was Donna proclaiming she was getting well. I took a deep breath, collapsed on my bed and fell to sleep. I was startled out of sleep from a bad dream and laid trembling and sweaty. I wanted to ignore it, but couldn't; it was foreboding. I reached for my dream journal on the bedside table and scribbled down everything I could remember. When I heard the garbage truck, I was releived. *Whew, the black cat was gone.* Fridays are busy days at the restaurant and I decided since I was awake I'd go in early, but I couldn't get the dream out of my mind.

I'm in my sister's living room, which is in disarray — randomly scattered boxes everywhere. Chaos. Three of my aunts stare at me and say, "You have the same disease as your sister." I scream back at them, "I'm not my sister!" and run out of the house. In a scene that could have been from Dante's Inferno, eight-foot tall golden raptors relentlessly chase me down winding stairs, clawing and screeching while biting me on the butt. I barely escape — my sons and I are driving down a dirt road. The car abruptly stopped, we get out and run to a 7-Eleven quick shop where three dark-skinned men dressed white chef's hats and aprons greet us.

I thought about calling my sister to see if she was okay, but could not bring myself to do it. *Don't, don't.* I didn't call Friday, Saturday, or Sunday. I felt paralyzed, my fingers unable to dial her number. The following Monday I was stirred awake with a dream of a *naked baby Buddha, sitting cross-legged, its hand caressing a double-edged sword.* I didn't know what to make of that.

On my way back from the gym later that morning, my cell phone rang. "There is a problem at Donna's house," the office manager at the dealership told me in a concerned voice.

I raced to her house, dreading the worst. An ambulance and police car, lights flashing, were parked in front and the house was cordoned off with yellow tape: **Police Line Do Not Cross.** As I stepped out of my car, a neighbor rushed over to me and said, "No one can go in. I think something is terribly wrong." My knees buckled and the lady from next door caught me under my arms before I hit the ground. I knew before I knew.

A police officer approached, "Who are you?" he asked.

"This is my sister's house. Where is she?"

"I'm sorry," he said, then paused and shook his head, "she's dead."

"What?" I asked, barely able to get the words out.

"Well, her cleaning lady tried to get in the front door and it was locked, so she went around back and looked through the window. She saw a body lying on the bed and ran next door to call 911," he said.

The neighbor put her arms around me and held me upright. I was hyperventilating, barely able to breathe; my legs no longer supported my body. "What happened?"

"We can't tell for sure, there's a lot of blood, most likely suicide. We can't permit you to go inside."

The kind neighbor helped to her home. "I need to make some calls, may I use your phone?" Molly, the catering manager at the restaurant whom I trusted and loved like a daughter, answered. Within minutes, she was by my side, holding my trembling body, my tears trapped inside from shock. *Strange, all of a sudden and odd sense of relief washed over me.* I remember thinking; *maybe she's no longer suffering. Maybe she's finally at peace.*

A meeting scheduled that morning with Stan, my attorney and confidant, had to be changed, I needed to let him know what happened. Donna's dead, and the police want to talk to me. My hands shook and heart raced as I dialed his number, "I have some awful news. My sister is dead, apparently suicide. Molly's here, I'm not alone, and the police want to talk to me."

"I'm so sorry. Have Molly take you to my house and I'll meet you there."

Molly drove me to Stan's house and returned to the restaurant. In the meantime, he had called his cousin Patti, one of my best friends, to come be with me. For a few moments we sat together thunderstruck, without words, and then Patti said, "Where are the boys?" I cringed at the thought of telling them, shaking my head, "There's no need to take them out of school, they don't need to know yet."

Stan asked if I was all right, went back to work and assured me he'd be with me before the police arrived.

"Do you want me to take you home?" Patti asked.

"Oh no, I don't want to be alone."

"Let's go for a drive," Patti said with tears in her eyes. "Have you thought about what you are going to do with Donna's body? Did she ever tell you what she wanted?"

"I don't know? I'm not sure. Donna and I never talked about that, but I don't think she wanted to be in the family crypt. She loved the outdoors and nature. Maybe somewhere…"

Patti drove through some of the graveyards in Wichita; I didn't know most of them. Driving through the meandering lanes felt surreal—I was half there and half somewhere else. As we turned into the Maple Grove Cemetery, I pointed to the tall red urn where our paternal great grandparents—emigrants from East Germany were buried. "I think this one is the most beautiful in Wichita." The caretaker saw our car and waved, Patti stopped, "Come to visit your kin?" he asked.

"No my sister died, and I wondered if there are any plots available."

"Oh dear, I'm sorry to hear about your sister. I guess you didn't know, there's a space next to your great grandmother," he said. *The steel plates in my shoulders loosened.* I remember stories about an eccentric little German woman who threw Christmas presents at the wall if she was in a bad mood. I looked at Patti and said, "I think we've found Donna's resting place."

Later that afternoon Patti drove me to my car, and followed me home. We began calling family and friends. Our voices were stressed and neither of us sounded like ourselves. Soon my other friends Margalee and Nickie arrived. I felt safe with them near.

Stan cancelled his afternoon meetings and was at my home with the police investigator arrived. We went into my study, closed the door, and the detective explained, "I'm here to interview you as a possible murder suspect. It's standard procedure, ma'am, because you're the next of kin." I suppose I should have been aghast, but I was so numbed by then that his statement didn't seem out of line. Nevertheless, I was thankful Stan was with me.

"How did she die?" I asked, wanting and not wanting to know.

"Do you really want the details?" he said with a pained expression.

I closed my eyes, shook my head, and mumbled. "Not really, but my attorney says we do."

"She used a dull kitchen knife, first stabbing herself in the side, then pubic bone, and finally slashed her wrists, neck and stabbed her heart."

I became dizzy, nauseous, and faint, barely able to grasp the horrific event. I ran to the bathroom gagging with dry heaves. Pain gripped my heart, *this can't be happening. This can't be true.* Resting my elbows on the edge of the sink, I splashed cold water on my face before returning to the room. *Why couldn't she have taken sleeping pills?* The detective looked into my eyes and said apologetically, "We had to question you first. After a full inquiry I'm sure it will be ruled a suicide." He stood, nodded and shook Stan's hand, then cupped my hands in his. Despite his rough skin, his touch conveyed compassion. "I'm real sorry, ma'am."

I was worried about telling my sons. In the past four years, we had buried their grandfather, grandmother, and great-grandmother and I was afraid another funeral might be too much. *How much do I tell them? I'll know when I see them.* I heard Garrett's voice as he stepped off the school bus. *He's such a cheerful boy.* "Hi, Mom. Why is everyone here?" I gave him a hug and whispered, "Something really sad has happened — your Aunt Donna died." He pushed me away and bolted out of the screen door — wailing — running to the neighbors, where he'd spent many hours while I was working. Trying to garner strength to comfort him, I slowly walked next door. When he saw me, he ran sobbing into my arms.

Justin and his girlfriend got home around six. After I told him, they disappeared in his '91 *Mercury Cougar*. He's not one to easily cry. I was thankful his girlfriend was with him. When he returned a few hours later, I put my arms around his lanky six-foot frame and asked, "How are you doing?"

He winced. I could tell he was shaken. "Driving calms me, helps me think. I drove past Donna's house. It's creepy. Do you think this is what the black cat meant?"

I shrugged, "Who knows? I'm just grateful she's not tormented anymore."

Garrett had run to the neighbors. Justin had driven around town. I wanted to flee: the city, the country, my DNA. Were it not for Justin and Garrett, I might have suffered the same fate as my siblings.

Those "it takes a village" friends gathered in my living room that Monday afternoon and evening, April 21, 1997, making calls, bringing food, listening and loving us. Patti, Margalee, Nickie, Mariti, Kim, Andy and other cherished ones sat trying to grasp the enormity of the experience. There is no judgment no right or wrong just despair and sorrow.

I was glad my parents were not alive. Losing two children out of three to suicide would have been too much to endure. I didn't cry that evening, I don't know why. My once playful sister whom I nicknamed *Queenie*, was naïve and childlike unable to live in the harsh world. She had become a ghost of herself, her brain snarled by twenty years of prescription drugs. Only after her death did I finally comprehend her psychosis; her life of unbidden voices impossible to will away, her life of dark pain and inertia.

That first night I got down on my hands and knees and prayed for respite and mercy — for Donna, for me, for my sons. The next morning my bathroom scale registered four pounds lighter than the day before. I showered for an hour, trying to scrub the image of my sister stabbing herself from my mind. My body quivered with revulsion. I brushed my skin raw with a coarse loofah.

I could not stop thinking about the dream I'd had a few days earlier and its haunting decree, *"You have the same disease as your sister."*

"I am not my sister!" The dreamer's retort was not reassuring. *Why were those three aunts there anyway?* Was I comparing them to Shakespeare's Three Witches in *Macbeth* who brew chaos, conflict and darkness, and foretell impending doom? I was angrier at the dream than Donna. *Do I really have the same disease as my sister?*

So many details I had yet to do, more calls to family and friends, mortuary, flowers. Decisions I would have to make as to whether or not to have an open or closed casket. What should she wear? Church? Minister? Writing the obituary? Her will? Her house? No time to mourn or feel pain...I had too much to do. Thank Heavens.

SUICIDE, again. Stark. Harsh. Cruel. Life gone amuck. No embellishment, death at its most raw. She did not leave a note. I assume her call six days ago to tell me she was okay was her way of saying goodbye.

She lay dead in her house for three days before being discovered. A friend called and told me, "The Tibetans say the body must lie unmoved for three days in order for the soul to fully depart." Knowing that helped lessen my guilt for not calling her for three days—slightly. Then I realized had I checked on her I might have been the one to find her body. I don't know if I could have lived with that. My friend told me divine compassion was at work after all. I believed her.

I did not want to hide the cause of her death. We had done that with my brother's in 1974, which left our family scarred by the stigma of suicide. But now there was no shame—mental illness, the nether world of psychosis and schizophrenia was to blame. The obituary stated Donna's cause of death as self-inflicted. It made crazy sense even though her method was unfathomable. I reconciled it as a courageous act of desperation; still, I worried who might be next, my sons or me? I hadn't begun to contemplate the impact her final act would have on any of the three of us.

Considering her morbid wounds, I chose a closed casket, but should it be open for viewing for family and close friends? I didn't know if even *I* dared look. The mortician gently touched my shoulder as we stood outside the viewing room and said, "Pam, I will stand right beside you. It's important you see her, otherwise you will wonder the rest of your life." He ended by saying, "We made her look good." I tiptoed in, braced myself in front of her casket, and cautiously peered at her puffed up body, dressed in her favorite long-sleeved blue and brown plaid shirt, turtleneck underneath to hide her wounds, bandaged wrists crossed over her heart barely visible. *Thank god, I listened to his wise counsel.* Yes, it was right to see her. I bent down and kissed her forehead, which was firm and cold, her soul no longer present. My mask of stoicism vanished—I could not hold back my sadness and pain. I sobbed, my eyes red rimmed from lack of sleep, and whispered, "Goodbye, sweet one. I hope you're at peace. I love you."

I realized the Donna I loved and knew as a sister had died long ago from the slow cruel torment of insanity. What the mortician couldn't know is that I would for years be haunted by Donna's violent act. Suicide leaves no resolution for relatives. We can only speculate. It irrevocably changes lives. Questions linger in unconscious darkness–nightmares recur.

Margalee and Nickie helped me choose a church where the minister would deal mercifully with suicide. I knew that George Gardner would be the right minister for the service; our spiritual beliefs were compatible. What I did not know was that George had three close family members commit suicide. His inherent understanding comforted me. As I was sitting in his office planning my sister's service he asked, "Did you know Donna came for counseling last week?"

My eyes widened, "No," I said. "Last time I talked to her, she told me she was getting well, but I didn't really believe her and didn't know what to say or do."

"Donna asked me if the Devil was real. I told her Evil exists. She told me the Devil had been talking to her and I told her to call the next time she heard from him, but she never called," George continued.

"Donna was staying at our aunt and uncle's house last week. She asked Aunt Mandy the same questions," I said.

George took my hand and said, "Bless you all. I know your sweet aunt and that she lost her first-born son to suicide years ago. Please tell her there is *nothing* anyone could have done to prevent this. It was Donna's way of healing her terror."

I do not remember the color of the sky or texture of the air that April day of her funeral and burial, my own life so occluded by shock, guilt, fear. The tones of my life were now being shaped by the shades of her death. I have only faint recollection of her burial; more memories of sitting in the front pew at College Hill United Methodist, my sons on either side of me, Donna's closed walnut casket covered with cascading white roses and calla lilies. Reverend George Gardner addressed my sons in a tender way by leaving his lectern to be near them as he talked about suicide. "Justin. Garrett. Your Aunt Donna loved both of you more than anything in her life. If she could have chosen another way, she would have.

Her pain was intolerable. Suicide was her only way out." He spoke of his own family's suicides, and his addressing suicide directly was crucial in helping the community mourn Donna's courageous, mysterious, and yet horrifying death. An invisible loving presence embraced us all.

Garrett sat nestled between Aunt Mandy and me in the back seat of the black limo on the way to the cemetery, his head cradled on my shoulder. He whispered, "I see sparkles." Aunt Mandy and I looked at each other. We felt a presence, a shimmering of light hovering, dancing. Our skin tingled. "Aunt Donna is with us. She's at peace now," we told him.

As Donna's disease progressed, the un-traversable chasm between us widened. She did not include me in her will, which meant I wasn't allowed in her house. Already overwhelmed with conflicting emotions, her declaration felt like one more slap in the face. I was hurt and furious, but I did possess the only key to her house. So, before I gave my key to the bank handling her affairs, Justin, Garrett and I "trespassed." I needed to be inside to see what was there. Garrett wanted her leather couch, I said, "NO." Someone had cleaned it, but there were still traces of blood. We didn't take anything that evening, but I called three of my aunts, the same three that had been in the dream, and asked them to meet me at Donna's house the following day—before the bank took possession and changed the locks. The bank's plan was to hold an estate sale. They told me if I wanted anything of my sister's or the family heirlooms, I would have to buy it—just like everyone else. The next afternoon, Justin, Garrett and I helped my aunts fill their cars with my grandmother's quilts, Donna's teapots and ceramic cups that she had made, my mother's hand written recipe book, kitchen accoutrements, and souvenirs. I took nothing, afraid the family curse, if it was a curse, might reside in her objects.

A few months later, after I had arranged for my sister's head-stone to be placed at her grave, something still felt incomplete. My parents and brother were in the marble mausoleum and my sister was in the ground by herself, even though buried next to our great-grandmother. I wanted my family to be together in death. My mother loved red oaks, so I planted one at my sister's gravesite, shading a bronze plaque dedicated to my sister, brother, mother and father. Donna's marble headstone with images of her ceramic bears engraved on either side reads:

"She Walks in Beauty"

Donna Jean Schmid

July 28, 1950 — April 21, 1997

Donna's suicide hung over me in the crevices and recesses of thought. I lived in two worlds simultaneously: my every day duties of mother, friend, restaurateur and my shrouded interior world of unanswerable questions, anxiety and raw emotions. The grief of suicide is different: there is no straight pathway or map to understanding, no predictable stages. It is composed of overwhelming guilt, unbidden feelings and thoughts mired in the quicksand of fear and confusion.

Like Justin the night I told him Donna had died, I needed to drive. Hoping distance and vistas would provide solace from the blinding emotional pain left by grief's serpentine path winding itself through my life, my children's lives. A month after Donna's death, I wound my way through the rolling Flint Hills of Kansas. The air was pungent, the land burned black to promote new growth. Vast clear skies overhead loosened the vice on my shoulders and the feeling of spaciousness in these lands my ancestors had trodden a century ago caressed me.

In the midst of this splendor, I heard for the first time the poet Rainer Maria Rilke's words:

Be patient toward all that is unsolved in your heart.
Try to love the questions themselves
Do not now seek the answers

Which cannot be given
Because you would not be able to live them and
The point is to live everything.
Live the questions now
Perhaps you will then gradually
Without noticing it live along some distant day
Into the answers.
–Rainer Maria Rilke, *Letters to a Young Poet*

The next morning I copied Rilke's poem on heavy bond with calligraphy pen, trimmed the edges with pinking shears and have kept it on my many desks through the years. The paper is now yellowed, the words still clear.

Coda:

Memorial Day, 2010. Justin and Garrett called from Wichita, they were on their way to the cemetery bearing white daisies to place on their Aunt Donna's grave. She had been dead thirteen years.

I used to see my sister's alabaster skin, blond hair and blue eyes in others—appearing unbidden like a mirage in the desert, for a moment or for days, until my projection dissolved. Early on, she visited in dreams showing me she was okay. Her apparition reminded me of Julie Andrews in *The Sound of Music;* arms outstretched twirling on the mountaintop in a white pinafore, her blond braids flying. I do believe she's at peace. Like the mystery of the black cat, I bow in reverence to the beauty and terror of the mysteries of life and death.

Nepal, 2005
Garrett, Pamela, Justin
"Where's the dot?"

Epilogue

This story may not have been written were it not for Mary's call three years ago, "Would you be a part of this project and tell your stories? Please write a hundred pages and bring them to Santa Fe." With thirty roughly written pages in hand, a story of theft and my brother's death, I met new friends ready to bare all.

I hadn't intended to write this story. It evolved organically out of many others, their threads connected in labyrinthine ways. My adult life has been shaped and inhabited by the lightening-like deaths of my brother and sister, their ghosts lurking in the shadows of my awareness. *Wasn't it time for me to be at peace with their deaths, let their lives and deaths be theirs and live my life forward?*

I've never been afraid to talk about my feelings; writing them was another matter. So I began. In stillness, a gurgling fountain outside my front door, I sit with my hands to my head like Rodin's "The Thinker" and wait—for the phrase, the right words to appear. Sometimes it happens while soaking in the bath, or walking my dog along the water's edge or awakening to dawn's light. As if magic, the workings of memory and psyche spiral upon each other finding their own groove on the page. I keep pad and pen in every room. Some memories seem as raw as their first blush; others are like aged photographs, cracked and faded, better left that way. I like to think I'm past this now, the suffering and rage dissipated to but an echo reverberating in the distance.

Like the whirlwind of Donna's death, this story has taken a village to write. I've had many conversations with Mary—reading what we had written to each other, listening between, asking questions. Memoirs about suicide and madness I hadn't dared read before became my psyche's nourishment. I voraciously devoured story after story, relating to the painful experiences of others helped validate, explain and make tolerable mine. I joined a Thursday morning memoir group, their encouragement, friendship and critique invaluable. I am fortunate and appreciative to have had so many friends and teachers read, comment on and hold dear this story.

Donna's suicide eclipsed almost everything early on; my sons and I were unraveled. In writing "She Walked in Beauty," our lives have been re-purposed, rewoven into the fabric of the living. I'm reminded of one of Justin and Garrett's favorite childhood books: *If You're Afraid of the Dark, Remember the Night Rainbow.*

Pamela Schmid Bjork

Pamela

Ronna Mee Brand

"You're the only Jewish Princess
I know who works," my comedian friend teases.

I belonged to Paul and Deena and two days before my first birthday, brother number one arrived; ten years later number two came along and took center stage. We grew up in Beverly Hills and were provided the best in life. Mom, bearing a strong resemblance to *Auntie Mame*, made sure of it. Her credo: "Life is a banquet, grab your plate and no matter the odds, never, ever give up!" Regretfully, I didn't follow her lead early on. The trauma of my first love's suicide made me reconsider her wise advice; I settled down and married my Jewish prince. Yet sadly, that too ended. Although I studied fashion design, art and psychology, nothing prepared me for life as a divorcee. Listening to Mom's/Mame's wise words and with and entrepreneurial spirit, I reinvented myself once more and became a successful Realtor. Life has awarded me wonderful friends, remarkable personal and business experiences and an exciting lifestyle. However, I will never forget my childhood allowance—seven dollars, and no matter how keenly I negotiated, it remained—seven. For parents who taught me the meaning of core values, I am grateful and I wear my tiara proudly.

Eve—N—More

By

Ronna Mee Brand

"Fasten your seatbelts; it's going to be a bumpy night!"
All About Eve,
Joseph Manckewicz, 1950

"*H*ey girl, it's Jack. Gotta quick question and I think I already know the answer. Did you give my phone number to anyone?"

"Of course not." *I was quite curious as to why he'd call and ask me that.*

"You'll never guess who called last night and on my *private* number."

"Who?"

"Eve."

"*Eve*? How did she get your number? Not from me...what did she want?"

"She started with how fabulous I am," he laughed. "Then she ended by saying, 'Ronna owes her success to you.' Then, acting coy took it a step further and suggested, 'Since I am a newbie, could you give *me* some guidance too?'" He snickered and continued. "She said, 'How about you and I get together for a cocktail? Here's my home phone.'"

I was outraged! "Holy shit, do you want me to find out how she got your number? And while I am at it, what the hell do you think she's up to?"

"Nah," he replied. "Let's see if she calls again."

Having a good sense of Jack, and knowing he loves the attention of women, this was a cautionary warning. He is someone for whom I hold the highest regard; he's a mentor, a dear friend, and I trust his instincts. Throughout the years, he's helped me with real estate dilemmas where his knowledge was invaluable. He brought me into his inner circle, so when it came to matters of a more personal nature, I never hesitated looking to him for answers.

Real estate in Beverly Hills, Bel Air and Holmby Hills isn't purchased by novices, or for folly. The deals are big–money by the truckload changes hands daily–and as a sole proprietor in this competitive, fast-paced arena, I've developed a "why not, do it" attitude which encompasses every aspect of my life. "Hard work" is my mantra, and mutual respect for my clients and peers is, I believe, the *key* to success.

My home is perched over a beautiful canyon with sweeping vistas just off the prestigious Mulholland Corridor. It's my sanctuary, and it's all mine! I live in the serene and peaceful Hollywood Hills and love it. I work in Beverly Hills and couldn't ask for more.

It was the mid 1980's, and my office was located in the Platinum Triangle, an ultra exclusive enclave well known for trendsetting boutiques and superstar-chef restaurants. Paparazzi stalked celebrities in the eternal sunshine, and the glamour of it all still captivates tourists who then become customers and clients. Sidewalk café conversations, beauty salon gossip and barstool chatter continue to fascinate.

Brand Realty, to my good fortune, was located in a building called "The Courtyard." The building boasts a beautiful

European garden, with office space on both sides of the entrance, and a glass-enclosed elevator in the center of the building, plus, the location exemplifies perfection. I used a palette of beige, white and black as the color scheme for the interior décor: basic, bold, *au courant*. My desk, the first enticement greets clients, and has become the subject of curiosity and conversation. It was commissioned and custom-built in China to specification; finished in black lacquer, hand-made ivory figurines and carved jade leaves. A coordinating four-paneled screen, the same motif as the office, formed a backdrop. Definitely good *Feng Shui*. Though my exclusive space lacked visible street frontage, it was adjacent to the inner atrium and situated furthest back in the complex. It didn't matter, Brand Realty had the right address for my business card because it was on the right street, Canon Drive, *aka* "Real Estate Row." "Location, location, location." Supporting this desirable office and incurring massive business overhead, not counting my home mortgage and upkeep, depletes an inordinate amount from the gross earnings. Maintaining an impressive office is a must, and the surest way to make an exceptional first impression.

I loved beautiful homes, meeting interesting people, and showing properties of the 'Rich and Famous'. "The Art of the Deal,"[3] to quote a certain icon, offered by far the biggest adrenaline rush and was what sold me on real estate as my calling. Between myself, seven agents and Victoria, our office manager, we needed to close as many sales as possible.

As in any business, success was predicated on maximizing income and minimizing expense. Anything left over at the end of the month determined how well I'd live or how I'd get by during down swings. It was the nature of the business.

I understood how important first impressions were to prospective clients evaluating whether they would work with me. Potential patrons assess a broker's status by a proper manicure, impeccable shoes and matching purse, and a car that screams success.

Just after I moved in, a new and cutting-edge hair salon opened. To make the equation even better, a trés chic eyewear

---

3 The Art of the Deal by Donald Trump, Warner Books, 1989

boutique opened down the street, with Valentino, Nina Ricci and Chanel feeding my out-of-control sunglass habit. What more could a working gal ask for?

As with many things in life, there can be a flip side to the blessings that come to us. When 'Eve' came along, I got a huge dose of *that* reality.

A mutual friend introduced us and from the moment we met, we hit it off—so much so, that my boyfriend BB and I included her in many of our activities; we became a traveling trio. There were invites to chic parties and impulsive getaways almost every weekend. Often the jaunts were to BB's home in Palm Springs with barbeques for 20 or more guests. Trips to La Jolla were even more elaborate. A gang of us would pile into a limo and head across the border to Rosarito Beach in Baja for a fresh lobster dinner. This adventure and rowdy group ended the evening by throwing the empty red crustacean carcasses and leftovers at each other in a food fight.

The good times were now better because I finally had the 'sister' I always wanted; I sensed the feeling was mutual. My pal Eve and I were similar in many ways. She was my height, had a spunky personality, a kinda Beverly D' Angelo overbite and a cute, though more curvaceous, figure. Our friendship grew closer and over time, we became the best of friends.

My career continued to climb—big time. Closing escrow after escrow. Eve, who'd been strictly involved in my social life, was an aspiring, but struggling actress. She knew my business was burgeoning, and it wasn't long before she approached me with, "Will you teach me real estate? I see how successful it is, and who better than you to teach me the ropes? Besides, we can work together; we can be a team!"

What a great idea! "Let's do it."

I started my company alone and except for necessary networking, I didn't spend much social time with colleagues from other offices. I felt it crucial to keep a mystique of success. The less competition knew, the more my accomplishments grew. The other agents working for me were nice, but older, so Eve, my contemporary, was the answer to my loneliness. Although I had Jack in the wings, I never had a full-time 'me,' which helped make the biz much easier for Eve. Her proposition was ideal and I couldn't wait to share all I'd learned. "I'll be happy to teach you everything I know, and when you get your license, you'll be able to make some 'real' money. I know quite a few actors who supplement their incomes this way. How exciting!"

Not only did I now have a business pal who'd be a great companion and also a confidant, I would also be a mentor to her, and I loved sharing my professional savvy and tricks of the trade. She got her license without a hitch and became a full-fledged agent of Brand Realty, Inc. Following me around like a puppy and acting the part of an ambitious, go-getter agent, Eve was learning the true heart of the business. Teaching her the ropes didn't stop at my office or viewing properties on caravan.

We went everywhere together — cocktail parties, mixers, industry dinners, seminars, conferences, and venues. Oftentimes our photos appeared in the newspaper. She mingled with my friends and total strangers with ease. The actor 'Eve,' proficient at improvisation and an intuitive mimic, picked up every fine point of a person's characteristics and mannerisms on the first take. It wasn't long before my 'newbie' agent graduated from gaining inspiration to emulating me. It started innocently, but when I noticed she was wearing the same Stuart Weitzman high heels which had become sorta my trademark shoe brand, I wondered, *how could she afford them? I still have to buy them when they're on sale.* I'm 5'3" and love high heels, *now she's making them part of her signature look too.* Within weeks she was sporting the same designer sunglasses, changed her hair color to the same shade and style, and there were some other weird copycat activities. *Hmmm, I'm not sure I like this.*

As I was leaving the office, I picked up my sunglasses, put them on and headed out the door.

"Hey Ronna, those are my glasses," she snapped.

"Oh sorry, I thought they were mine. They look like mine."

When looking back on that situation, I couldn't believe I didn't pick up on what was really going on. Red lights flashed all around me; I can only surmise, I didn't want to notice.

I happened to be updating my scrapbook and press clippings when a friend dropped by. She picked up one of the photos and said, "Oh my god!"

"What, what is it? Let me see."

The photo that made her gasp, taken in 1986 at the christening of a luxury hotel in Palm Springs where Prince Charles was the guest of honor, was Eve and me, dressed to the nines, and standing between us, handsome as ever, Tony Curtis. My friend was stunned by the similarity between Eve and me. We looked like bookends; everything was identical. "We made quite a threesome, don't you think?"

"Are you kidding?" she replied. "Wow, I think that's eerie. What was going on?"

Eve went a step further and started to incorporate words and phrases I said. If I had a nickname for someone, she adopted it. She went as far as sounding exactly like me when she'd answer the phone "Brand Realty, may I help you." People thought they were talking with me. *Shit, she's now imitating my speech!*

At first, it was flattering. *She must think highly of me to try to emulate me.* That turned out to be a bunch of crap. Little did I know the pedestal she'd put me on had a trap door over an alligator pit. It didn't take long before Eve represented her first client on a property sale, her first escrow. My responsibility as her broker was making sure there were no complications. However, I was becoming concerned she was getting too close to Christine, the agent representing the seller. *Uh-oh, they are mixing business with pleasure.* As Eve was leaving for the day she said, "Christine and I are going to a bar and dancing tonight," in a flippant bragging tone. It seemed odd that she didn't include me, but I shrugged it off. "Who cares?" But, my experience told me she was heading down a problem-filled path. Frustrated, I thought about the approach I'd take, wanting to keep a mild tone, yet definitive — you should refrain from spending social time with Christine until your deal closes. When I spoke with her she said, "You can't tell me who to be friends with."

"Look, I'm not saying that, but you are jumping into a situation that could cost you the deal, and put the company in a questionable light. Your friendship with this woman has gone from business to social at lightening speed, and you don't know if you can trust her."

"Ronna, I know what I'm doing," she said with insolence.

I felt like slapping her. *Who does she think she is? She works for me, and what is this snotty attitude?* I handcuffed myself and let it slide convincing myself she was trying to show her independence. *Can't she see what this agent is up to?* It was obvious that Christine was prying her for information trying to get a 'home court' advantage. Eve was still 'green' and too conceited to realize. Two days later, Christine — Eve's newest best friend — reported her to Brand Realty for a wrongdoing in the conduct of business. Eve had broken a cardinal rule in real estate: a buyer must be accompanied by their agent when viewing a property. Eve handed her clients the keys and told them it was okay to go inside.

I salvaged and smoothed out the issue with great care so as to not lose my business I'd worked so hard and diligently to grow. This lesson in basic real estate practice left Eve with egg on her face. Feeling she'd learned her lesson, I didn't rub it in; I thought the embarrassment would be enough. However, this was far from the end of the many predicaments she'd instigate or entangle my business and personal life in, 'Eve-n-more.'

Soon my good friend Ben, my hairdresser, told me he was concerned that I was being too generous with my life and business relationships. "What do you mean?" I asked.

"Eve comes into the shop right after your appointments and she always requests the same look and color I've created for you; I think you may want to pay attention to this."

"You know, Ben, I've got to tell you, you're not the first person who's noticed Eve's bizarre behavior." I told him the 'Eve' situation was getting worse. Lee, a girlfriend since childhood, called and told me Eve was inviting herself over to hang out. Lee didn't particularly like Eve and said she was alerting me. Seems too, little Eve was doing "blow" and Lee was completely turned off by that. *God, how clueless can I get?*

The camaraderie between Eve and me holding so much promise was becoming distorted and dysfunctional and starting to get to me.

The next incident became a real issue. Each year, I looked forward to the traditional Halloween soiree hosted by my friend Patty. The same close friends were always invited. I relish her delicious chicken enchiladas, and everyone brings a favorite dish. This year instead, I brought a mixed tape of scary music—howling wolves, creaking doors, and blood curdling screams. Patty's home not only sounded, but also looked freaky, covered in spider webs. Weird jack-o-lantern's lined the walk to the front door, and ghosts hanging from trees, swayed in the breeze. We took turns carrying cauldrons of Butterfingers, Snickers, M&M's and Hershey bars when the trick-or-treaters rang the bell. When Eve found out about the party, she said, "Do you think I could go with you?" begging like a child. *What a mistake.* After a few too many libations, she wandered outside saying she wanted to see all the kids and their costumes. When she returned, she'd picked up a couple of grimy-looking guys who smelled like cigarettes and booze. *What is she thinking? Who knows what these guys are up to and she brings them into Patty's house?*

Patty, always demure, wasn't so demure. Without hesitation, she told them they would have to leave immediately.

I wanted to kick them out myself, having brought Eve. I felt responsible and was mortified. I made apologies, grabbed Eve's arm, and left the party. Jack who was an attendee caught my eye, and nodded his head.

When I arrived at my office the next morning a beautiful bouquet greeted me...*wonder who sent these?* The note inside read, "That was quite an 'Eve-n-ing'...Jack."

It seemed there would have to be a sizeable *last straw* or a very large bucket of cold water thrown in my face to wake me up so I could see what was going on. I believe in karma and would not wish anyone misfortune. However, this chapter in my life was becoming a nightmare.

Someone recently asked me after hearing about Eve and her antics, "Did you see the movie, *Single White Female?*"

When I imagine how much worse her obsessive behavior could have become, the thought is chilling. I consider myself lucky. Though my heart may have been in the right place, my brain was somewhere else. I was dumbfounded that I was the only one who didn't see Eve's manipulation. I learned her drug problem may have contributed to her behavior. If so, why didn't she ask for my help? Again, I'm rationalizing.

I recall the day when Victoria, my office manager, finally hit me over the head. "Ronna," she said. I give you at least $300 to $500 hundred a week, cash, and lately you've been asking for more."

"You're right, I hadn't given it much thought until now, but every time I look into my wallet the money's gone."

"Something's up, and I don't like it," she said. "You don't squander. Where's it going? Do you have this week's cash receipts?"

Opening my wallet, I had a few, but they didn't add up to amount Victoria had given me.

"Shit, I'm almost out of money again. Can you go to the bank and get some, Vic?"

Tuesday is Caravan Day, the day Realtors view the new homes on the market. Before leaving, Victoria motioned for me to come into the back area by the coffee pot. "This can't wait," she said. "Put these bills–$500 in one hundred dollar bills – in your wallet. Just do it."

Eve and the other agents arrived, and after a brief meeting, we headed out. Eve with me. She didn't know my radar was on. With so many houses to see in so little time, we'd leave our purses in the car, dash inside and out as fast as we could. At our first stop, Eve said, "I'm not interested in seeing this one, I'll wait for you here." I jumped out ran inside, saw it wasn't special and headed back to the car. When I got inside, she said, "Ya know, I've changed my mind. I think I'll take a look." I opened my wallet, and sure enough, a couple of the bills were missing. *Crap, she had to have taken them.* It was hard for me to act as though nothing had happened as we continued on to the other open houses. *How could she not see or feel my disappointment?* My mind started racing back over all the warnings I'd been given, *Patty, Jack, Ben, Lee, and now Victoria. Clothes, hair, sunglasses, shoes, co-opting my friends, invading my privacy, pretending to be me, and now stealing! Fuck, what am I gonna do?*

After caravan, we headed back to the office. Our talk was minimal. I rushed inside and looked at Victoria, holding my thumb up and nodding with a disgusted look on my face. She got it! The usual office meeting after caravan everyone got together and talked about their impressions of the new houses. I asked them to stay a minute. "It's been brought to my attention; some things have gone missing from purses and desks in the building. I recommend you keep a close eye on your belongings."

Eve acted indifferent. She didn't look surprised. *What did I expect? After all, Ronna, she's an actress. I even thought about offering her a second chance; help her if she had a problem…whatever, drugs, money. Was I nuts?*

We always ate at *La Scala* after caravan, both of us starving from gallivanting all over Beverly Hills. Their chopped salad filled us up, were healthy and low-cal. "Are you ready to go to *La Scala*?" I asked.

"Sure," she replied.

We headed out on the short walk across the courtyard. *The flowerbeds look exceptionally vibrant today.* By the time we got on the corner of Canon Drive, I was about to explode. Everything I heard and saw seemed exaggerated and got bigger as we waited for the light to change before we could cross the street. No longer able to keep quiet, I asked, "Is there something you want to tell me?"

"No, what are you talking about?"

"The money, Eve, the money." I said. "Would you like to try and see if we can work something out? Are you in trouble?"

Eve was wearing black sunglasses. It was a though I was looking in a mirror, confronting myself. She pulled the glasses down her nose, peered over the top, glared at me and said, "Fuck you!" Then she made an about face and stomped off wearing <u>my</u> Stuart Weitzman's. Horrified, but not surprised by her rude behavior, I thanked god, she was gone, gone for good. I never saw her again.

To paraphrase a quote from Oscar Wilde,

Who is morally bankrupt? A person who knows the price of everything, and the value of nothing.

Jack and Ronna
"My mentor and my best friend."

Eve, Fred, and Ronna
"He's mine!"

Epilogue

"Hello."

"Ronna, it's Mary. Be careful what you wish for!" she said with a mischievous chuckle.

When meeting Mary a few years back, I learned she was writing a book. We had something in common: I was too.

"Would you like to join us and write a story for our book?" Mary asked. I was so flattered. There it was…*be careful what you wish for.*

I wanted to be a part of their project. *Could I make the grade?*

I would need to learn a new style of writing, pronto: memoir. The weight of the world was on my shoulders. Now, I would have to remember as best I could, events from thirty years ago. I couldn't let Mary down. *Talk about stress.*

With every draft, I relived my experiences with Eve.

I realized how fortunate I was to have friends who cared about my well-being during the tumultuous time when I was dealing with Eve. They tried to protect me from someone whom they felt was loaded with ulterior motives. Some have said they believe she was stalking me.

While writing my story, I learned a very big lesson. I've matured, am comfortable in my own skin and am proud of my professional reputation, which could easily have been destroyed by Eve's sinister and selfish motives. That being said, my antenna is up and I haven't been taken for a ride like that since — and I don't intend to allow anything like that to happen again.

Looking back, one thing was clear: Eve didn't realize you have to earn the loyalty of friends. The 'Eve Experience' solidified my beliefs about the importance of true friends. Patty continues her annual Halloween bashes and I'm still an invitee. BB and I enjoy a dinner now and then. My La Jolla pals still keep in touch. Victoria continues to mother me, and Ben colors my hair every six weeks. With great sadness, Jack passed away in 2010. He will forever be my best friend and mentor.

Was I stressed to the max? You bet. Was I challenged? To the nth degree. Was I meant to relive memories and make new friends? No question.

Ronna Mee Brand

Ronna

A Tribute to Katherine

By

Mary Beal Berchem

The casita was built in 2001 as an addition to the historic main house, which dates back to the 1800s. It's difficult distinguishing the vast age difference between the old and new since we re-stuccoed the pinkish-tan adobe a few years back. Many of the residences on Buena Vista Street are Santa Fe's version of row houses; ours is a bit more kept up than some. The maze type construction — purposeful accommodations for a Niño Nuevo or domitorio con Abuela. I've met folks whose families lived here fifty or more years ago and they know the Hispanic surnames of others going back generations. We bought it in 2004.

I was on a two-day quest to find the perfect house, a second home in Santa Fe—'*Corazon mi Corazon,*' heart of my heart. My husband Mike was all for it, however, he had two requirements.

"It must have a guest house we can rent and be within walking distance of a bar. I've always wanted to live in a neighborhood with a bar like the one in '*Cheers.*'"

The South Capital is my favorite area and I began driving up and down the narrow one-way streets looking for 'For Sale' signs. Finding the 'pied a Terre' perfect size, location and price, I knew it was the one. However, scrutiny revealed an 'In Escrow' sign on the ground, hidden among weeds. Though not dismayed, I called my realtor David.

"Mary, I remember it sold," he said.

"Do me a favor, call the listing agent and check," I asked.

Within twenty minutes, he called back, "Well your hunch paid off. It fell out Friday, and the agent didn't have time to pull it off the market. Do you want to see it?"

"Of course, it looks perfect — has a renter already, the *Dragon Room* is two blocks away and Mike will love it."

Serendipity played like a symphony, all went well and closing a breeze. I was as giddy as when I got my first bike, a bright metallic blue *Western Flyer*.

Surely, I thought, it was meant to be...*destiny*. I can tinker, pick apricots and apples from the trees in the yard, paint the walls bright lively Mexican colors — go wild. Santa Fe lets you do that.

The tenant's name was Katherine; she's quiet and quite pleased we want her to stay. I thought *we're the lucky ones*. In addition, and from all appearances, she was thoughtful and unassuming, *almost invisible*. Having had other renters whom were less than courteous, I want our relationship amiable, and by the way she talked, she took pride in the little casita. She had a plentitude of interesting flowers and herbs and liked my idea of planting water-conserving perennials. I wanted her to feel it is her home too; believing she will keep a vigilant eye on things gives me peace of mind.

I remember Mike commenting on her first water and sewer bill. "Look at this bill, Mary. How could she use so little?"

"Get used to it, that's Katherine, never over-stepping, or taking more than she needs."

Over the next six years, we developed a special bond, sharing childhood memories, talking about our former love relationships and friends, discussing metaphysical and esoteric philosophies, and disclosing a few secrets. We became confidants. I lived a much different life in Los Angeles and our house in Santa Fe — my sanctuary. Katherine's life appeared quite humble: home, 225 square feet, uses few, if any disposables, re-cycles; hand-washes her clothing and hangs on a wooden rack to dry. She drove an older faded black *Honda Civic*, and seemed to have a limited number of friends. Perplexed by her life of scarcity, I thought it somewhat odd at first–that is, until I got to know her.

Three days prior, I'd arrived from LA with my friend Ronna. Eager to show her the sites in *The City Different*, a name given to Santa Fe because it's like no other place—except for maybe Venice, Italy.

"I haven't stopped by to say hello to Katherine, I really should before I do anything else. Hey, Ronna, there's a store you're gonna love—*Jackalope*. It looks like a Mexican mercado, it's my *Toys R Us.*"

"Let's go," she said. "How long do I have to get ready?"

We were off, however, I forgot to stop by Katherine's to say hello.

Pulling into the gravel parking lot of *Jackalope* I felt as though I had time traveled back to a quaint Mexican pueblo. Outside, the mud-brown adobe building–complete with arches, bell tower, huge wooden door with hand-forged wrought iron pulls–remind me of an old mission. Inside, an explosion of color—vibrant yellows, cerise rose, aquas, and brilliant orange ceramic pots and tableware abound. New Mexican spices fill the air with aromas of chipotle, cumin and coriander. A CD plays Rubin Romero's serene, indigenous classic guitar, and *tchotchkies* from all over the world hang from the ceiling enveloping every inch of the warehouse-sized room.

Ronna's eyes lit up. "My kinda place," she said, heading off to shop. I stopped, amazed at the grand, Talavera figure—she's remarkable, I've never seen one so big or painted so exquisitly. A man's voice said, "She's a beauty; we've never had one that size before." I hadn't noticed him because I was so engrossed with the *Dia del los Muertos*, woman. "I'll take her," I said, without hesitation and not asking the price—*something rare for me!*

"Will she fit in your car? You'll need at least five feet" he said."

"Yeah, I think so."

The manager carefully wrapped her in bubble-wrap; we loaded her in the car, and headed home. Jerome, my handyman, was there and we carried her into the house. I began assembling the various body parts—twisting on arms, elongated boney hands with their bright red fingernails, and securing the bouquet of crepe paper Sunflowers–until everything was perfectly in place. Next, her garish head with its 'ear to ear' toothy smile slipped effortlessly on the neck vertebrae. An oversized verdant bonnet trimmed with blue, yellow, red, purple and white Talavera painted flowers crowned her skull. "At last she's home."

Having completed her assembly, we stood back admiring the statuesque skeleton woman.

"We should give her a name," Ronna said.

"How about Esmerelda? That's a romantic Latin name," I suggested. We all nodded our approval.

I felt awful because I didn't get over to say hello to Katherine that day. I noticed the light had been on over her gate since I'd arrived. That was unusual, but she'd been leaving it on since her stroke last year. That evening, I walked over, knocked on the gate, but she didn't answer. I thought she hadn't heard, so I went to the glass door and knocked. Again, no answer. H*mm, maybe she's out with friends.* Everything looked normal inside; nothing seemed out of place. The next morning I decided I was definitely going to say hello. The outside light was still on—*rare she hadn't turned it off during the day, with her strong beliefs about energy conservation.* After knocking, and no answer, I jiggled the doorknob; it wasn't locked. I stuck my head inside and called, "Katherine, hello?" Quiet. Feeling uncomfortable, I closed the door and went back to our house.

"What's up?" Ronna said.

"I don't know, but I think I better call Mike".

"You need to go inside, check each room, and call me back," he said.

This time Ronna came with me, but waited outside.

Everything looked okay; the room still has that odd odor from the vitamins, flower essences and natural botanicals and homeopathies she uses. The small drop leaf table covered with a brown-ochre and cream Zapotec rug, was minimally messy. Little 3x5 notes with scribbling like the ones she'd given me before, a magnifying glass and a couple of boxes full of rows of tiny blue dropper bottles, pens and paper clips strewn on top. However, no Katherine. The bathroom door was open and with some trepidation, I moved closer. There she was, sitting hunched over, motionless.

My first thought was, *maybe she fainted and passed out?* I was a little reluctant to touch her, but I knew I must. I put my hand on her upper back and pushed — adrenaline raced through my blood; her frail body was hard and cold. *Call Mike — I need to call Mike.* He answered on the first ring. "She's dead. What should I do?"

"Hang up and call 9-1-1."

"Ronna, I need you to stay by the phone. I've got to flag down the police, because they won't know where to turn."

Within minutes, Officers Jones and Chavez arrived. "Who are you, and where is the body?"

"She's back there," I said, pointing to the guesthouse.

Ronna and I waited outside, whispering, speculating and full of 'what-ifs.' I guess it was about fifteen minutes later when Officer Jones reappeared.

"What do you think happened?" I whispered.

"The preliminaries look like natural causes, but until an autopsy, we won't know for sure. Was she a happy person?"

Odd she'd ask that. Stepping closer, almost as though she didn't want anyone to overhear, "She must have been a tormented soul." Now, I understood. *She must have seen some of Katherine's notes.*

"Will you be contacting her next of kin?" I asked.

"I need to know the last time you saw her alive." Officer Chavez asked, "It has to be in my report."

"I was here two weeks ago; we went to a movie, she invited me in for a cup of tea, we talked for an hour and I left, that's the last time I saw her alive."

I will never forget that night after the movie. I can't imagine the look on my face when she revealed, "I've lived with this secret my entire life. I've only told one other person and I want to tell you." Horrified by her disclosure, I begged, "Please tell your story. We'll include it in the book."

"Let me think about it," she replied.

Her forlorn eyes always looked raw and irritated.

Reaching out she handed me a stack of small slips of paper. "Please take these notes; I want you to have them."

"What do you want me to do with them?"

"We'll talk when you come back," she said. I gave her a hug and left.

The Medical Examiner concluded her investigation and two assistants wheeled the gurney with Katherine's petite body, wrapped inside a heavy black bag, out of her home, but stopped before pushing it through the gate and said, "If you'd like to leave before we take her it's okay."

"I'm all right, but may I say goodbye?"

"Sure."

Bending over I put my hand where I thought her heart would be and whispered, "Good bye dear friend, sweet soul, rest in peace."

I thanked everyone and watched them leave. Ronna asked if I would drive her back to Jackalope, "I'd like to buy a few gifts to take home."

We barely spoke inside the car; then, as if cued by a director, we looked at each other and in unison blurted, "Let's change Esmerelda to Katherine."

"Of course, what a perfect tribute, she will be a beautiful reminder." I said.

Once inside *Jackalope*, Ronna went about shopping. Feeling drained, I sat near the fountain and waited. From out of nowhere, a man's voice: "Aren't you the lady who bought the *Dia del los Muertos?*" Waving his hand, he motioned to a woman on the other side of the store.

"Celia," he said. "This is the lady who bought the Talavera woman."

"Hello, I'm the buyer and Raoul told me about you. I'm so glad to meet you. I think you were meant to have her. Did he tell you I bought two and the other one broke?"

"It's ironic talking to you about this."

"Why?" she responded sounding perplexed.

"This morning I found my friend dead."

"Dios Mio, how awful. I'm sorry. Do you know about Dia de los Muertos? In Mexico, we honor our dead loved ones November 1; each skeleton figure represents those who have died, and we name them too."

Ronna made her purchases and came to where we were talking. Upon overhearing our conversation, interrupted, "We originally named her Esmerelda, but decided on the way here to change it to..." but, before she could finish, Celia interrupted her–

"Esmerelda's a beautiful name, but as I recall, that one's name is Katarina."

"What?" Our reactions identical–shock and disbelief.

"My friend's name was Katherine."

"See," she said, crossing herself three times, "It's a sign; you were meant to have her."

During our conversations, Katherine told me disturbing things, which made me angry and sad. She spent the years I knew her trying to regain her voice and sense of self. Her diligence meant hours alone, seeking, reading, and meditating much like a cloistered nun. By including her notes and telling this story, with hope, her voice will give aid to others who are victims of abuse. Our wish would have been that she lived to see her story told. Her words, succinct and deliberate, free her spirit and give encouragement to everyone who may have lost his or her voice through misuse or abuse. Fear, shame, and guilt only serve to continue the abuse, and protect the abusers.

During her last two years of life, she suffered a stroke, which makes reading some of the notes difficult. Nevertheless, the essence of meaning is clear and heartfelt.

Katherine gave me the following hand written notes, during our last visit in Santa Fe, New Mexico, 2010.

12/21 or 22 "It is a waste of a precious life for you to think you are not loved."

5/12/09

1. Focus on gratitude for each
of the small tasks I have
accomplished.
2. If have a little energy for
something but no room in my
head to ask nature about it, do
the task. EG: watering plants.

5/12/09
1. Focus on gratitude for each of the small tasks I have accomplished.
2. If have a little energy for something but no room in my head to ask nature about it, do the task. EG: watering plants.

8/1/07

DDP: to discover the source of my ongoing desire to die,

8/1/07 Soil-less ETS 60 drops MY MOTHER

DDP: to discover the source of my ongoing desire to die,
8/1/07 Soil-less ETS   MY MOTHER
60 drops

2/6/? I wanted so much to have a father, I tried to overlook his limitations

2/6 EoP for me
—to understand
what kind of a
person my father was

2/6/? EOP for me
—to understand
what kind of a
person my father was

2/7/10
EOP for me!
-the impact of
my father's criticism
of me.

2/7/10
EOP for me!
-the impact of
my father's criticism
of me.

7/6/? - EOP
My heart center

7/6/? EOP:
I have been
lethally injured

7/8
EOP!
my truth

7/8/?
EOP:
My truth.

8/15/? EOP:
I have been in - a state
of perpetual abuse for
my whole life.

9/8/?
suicide
I struggled with idea
of suicide so much.

9/12/10 EOP
I told my brother that
my
father terrorized me &
sexually abused me & 3X
sold me for sex to other men

8/8/? EOP
? Sold for sex
by father several times
with complicity of mother

5/6/10 EOP
Help me integrate
knowledge and
the understanding
I have of how my
my mother influenced me.

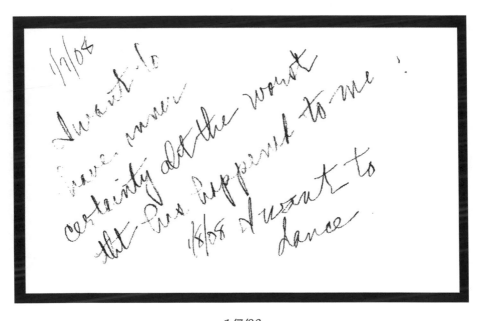

1/7/08
I want to have inner certainty abt the worst that has happened to me
1/8/08 I want to dance.

What to do abt my voice?

Dedication

To our mothers,

Helen (Deceased)

Polly Hansen (Deceased)

Dr. Ann Marilyn Rufer Shaeffer

Stachia Milner Feld (Deceased)

Dorothy M. Wombacher Starkey (Deceased)

Betty Goldberg Boyer (Deceased)

Frankie Jean Edmundson Schmid (Deceased)

Deena Ester Brand

Attributions

1. Jigsaw Puzzle

author: Pyson

source: Bing Images

Read other information related to keeping secrets

1. **Why Keeping A Secret Feels So Physically Burdensom**, The Huffington Post, By Amanda L. Chan, 3/25/2012

2. **Go Ahead & Spill the Beans: Tufts Researchers Prove Secrets are Physically Burdensome**, The Huffington Post, Tufts EDU, By Lauren Landry, Posted 3/27/2012

3. **The Physical Burdens of Secrecy**. Michael L. Slepian, E.J. Masicampo, Negin R. Toosi, Nalini Ambady, The Journal of Experimental Psychology: General, Mar. 5, 2012

4. **The UCLA Study on Friendship Among Women**

Special Thanks

Nola Foulston, District Attorney 18th Judicial District, Wichita, Kansas

Bella Mahaya Carter, Jayne Hamilton, Dottie Hillyer, Dr. Douglas S. Daniels, Estella Loretto,

Cherry Pickman, Carol Anne Seflinger, Kendall Sherwood, Suzanne Stanewich

Made in the USA
San Bernardino, CA
22 January 2013